Charles Sperling Cumberland

Sport on the Pamirs and Turkistan Steppes

Charles Sperling Cumberland

Sport on the Pamirs and Turkistan Steppes

ISBN/EAN: 9783743316126

Manufactured in Europe, USA, Canada, Australia, Japa

Cover: Foto ©ninafisch / pixelio.de

Manufactured and distributed by brebook publishing software (www.brebook.com)

Charles Sperling Cumberland

Sport on the Pamirs and Turkistan Steppes

PREFACE.

It is with some diffidence that I venture to offer the following pages to the public, and feel that a short explanation of my reason for doing so will not be out of place.

In the year 1889 I carried out a long-projected expedition from India *viâ* Kashmir, Chinese Turkistan, the Pamirs, and Asia Minor, and shortly after my return published a rather full journal in 'Land and Water.'

At that time very little was known of these regions, and still less interest taken in them, therefore all idea of writing a book on the subject was considered a work of supererogation. Since then, however, the Russian claims and expeditions to our frontiers beyond Gilghit have brought these parts into notice, and other writers have awakened interest in them.

As I happen to have covered a greater extent of country than that described by some more recent travellers, and, having frequently left the main caravan routes, have crossed passes and hunted over mountains which do not come in the way of an ordinary journey, I hope these descriptions of scenery and sport may still prove acceptable; and that my offering these pages somewhat late in the day will be excused: and I trust that the book may not be voted "a day behind the fair."

My thanks are due to the editor of 'Land and Water' for kindly returning my diary, thus enabling me to reproduce what appeared there in narrative form.

As regards the sport obtained, I was fairly successful, bringing back various specimens of the big game of Central Asia, comprising *Ovis poli*, red-deer of Turkistan, wild camel, jeran antelope, and, in addition to these, some of the game-birds of the country: also from Kashmir, markhor, ibex, burrel, &c.

The mapping was done by my companion, Captain Bower of the Indian Intelligence Department, who has since distinguished himself further in that line.

C. S. CUMBERLAND.

CONTENTS.

CHAPTER I.

IN KASHMIR.

PAGE

Shooting ibex in Kashmir—Expedition to Pangi—A night under a glacier—In the Chilas country . . . 1

CHAPTER II.

SPORTING WANDERINGS.

The pilgrim at the bridge—Shooting burrel—In the Pir Panjal after markhor—A narrow escape—Death of Rasaka—Return to Leh—Festival at a *gompa*—Across the Sasar and Karakoram passes—An oasis—*Ovis Ammon* and shapoo 11

CHAPTER III.

START FOR CHINESE TURKISTAN.

Preparations for trip to Chinese Turkistan and Pamirs—Procure a guide—Start with Captain Bower by the Scind valley—Baggage-pony drowned—Government interferes

—M. Dauvergne joins us—Climbing the Khardung Pass—The spot where Dalgleish was murdered—A court of inquiry 21

CHAPTER IV.

JOURNEY TO THE PAMIRS.

Hospitality of the Wakhis—A stiff climb—An unexpected friend—The Russian's camp—Plains of Turkistan—Distinguished visitors—We lose our way—A fertile valley—The Beg of Kargalik—A successful deal—Crossing the Yarkand river—A novel raft-propeller—The Hakim Beg awaits our arrival—A state visit—An awkward fall—First signs of *Ovis poli*—More interviews—The Taghdumbash Pamir—A wolf in the way—Changing ground . . 37

CHAPTER V.

AMONG THE PAMIRS.

We visit Dauvergne's camp—A successful stalk—Dead beat—Dauvergne leaves—The Kilik valley—A tantalising shot—Message from Gromchefski—An avalanche—Akal Jahn provides shikaris—More Oves—Bower's success—An ice wall—Collecting the spoils—Tea with Gromchefski 86

CHAPTER VI.

JOURNEY TO YARKAND.

A change of latitude—Fishing—A day with Younghusband—*En route* for Yarkand—Tagherma Peak—Sufferings of the ponies—Rufus succumbs—An awkward gorge—Across the Torak to the Charlung valley—Climbing a precipice—The Kara and the Kizil Dawan—An icy road—Midnight breakfast—A long tramp—The fort at last . . . 110

CONTENTS. ix

CHAPTER VII.

YARKAND.

A Turki's hut—Our villa residence—An awkward situation—
Visiting the Amban—Mahomed Unis makes us a present
—The return call—Refitting 125

CHAPTER VIII.

FROM YARKAND TO AKSU.

Touching farewells—Bower takes another route—On the
road to Maralbashi—A falcon party—Hospitable villagers
—A forest of the past—Shooting jeran—A musical Turki
spoils sport—A false alarm—Visited by a Chinaman—A
fine stag—The Yangi Hissar—A caravanserai—Tigers—
A message from Bower—Chillon—March to Aksu—
Mahomed Amin—A welcome *mazar*—The Tian Shan
mountains—An exciting gallop—Curious huts—Wild
camel 140

CHAPTER IX.

EXPEDITION TO KALMUK.

The legend of Takla Makhan—An unexpected shot—Arrival
of Bower—Comfortable quarters—A village dance—With
the Kalmuks—The Tunktchi makes difficulties—Above
the region of wood—Frozen out—The Khan's mother—
Return to Shah Yar—A wild swan—A deer-drive—Back
at Aksu—Chinese court of justice—Summary punishment
—Giving a lesson—A friendly escort—The Chunkoo's
band—Fresh hunting-grounds—*Ovis Carolini*—Across
the steppes—Imperial grouse—Kashgar . . . 175

CHAPTER X.

KASHGAR TO THE KARAART PAMIR.

The capture of Dad Mahomed—Europeans at Kashgar—A fresh start—By the river Uluart—Across the Kosh-beli Pass—The poli disappear—A long shot . . . 224

CHAPTER XI.

THE KARAKUL PAMIR—AND HOME.

In Russian territory—A stern chase—Found dead—Hard hit—An ice raft—Finished at last—A wild lot—An adventurous lady—We lose the caravan—A sad parting—The Tengiz-bai Pass—At the custom-house—A ridiculous mistake—Marghilan—Breaking up the caravan—Journey by *tarantass*—Return to civilisation 239

INDEX . . 275

SPORT ON THE PAMIRS AND TURKISTAN STEPPES.

CHAPTER I.

IN KASHMIR.

SHOOTING IBEX IN KASHMIR — EXPEDITION TO PANGI — A NIGHT UNDER A GLACIER—IN THE CHILAS COUNTRY.

THERE is a disease—the Germans call it *Wanderlust*—which no time can cure, however much the subject when on the tramp may vow " This trip must be the last." Shooting is losing its charm, the pleasure of killing does not compensate for the pain of missing, the petty annoyances of camp-life irritate, and he determines to give it up.

The trip finished, he goes home; at the end

of a week the decision appears to have been too abrupt; a little farther north, south, east, or west, matters would have been better. In a fortnight he is keen to be off again, and in three weeks has settled the details of another expedition.

So it was with myself. For many years I had enjoyed varied sport in the Himalayas; then my thoughts turned towards exploring new lands, and hunting the monarch of the mountains, the grand *Ovis poli*, or Marco Polo's sheep. Before this could be achieved, however, much had to be done. I propose, therefore, to relate some of my experiences in the Himalayas which led to these further wanderings.

Being on leave one year, I went to Kashmir, though without any particular object in view. No sooner had I arrived, however, than the shikaris fell upon me as vultures on their prey, hovering round from dawn till dark. "The sahib had a rifle; why did he not take a nullah and shoot ibex?"

When I had been in the valley about a week, it struck me I might do worse; so, engaging little Rama, now one of the best shikaris in Kashmir, we made a start. All the best nullahs or valleys being taken, I had to content myself

with the Gwi, a little nullah running into the
Wardwan. How well I remember my first day
on the ibex-ground! My feelings were far from
comfortable. The *kuds* looked horribly dangerous; there was nothing to hold on to except an
occasional bramble, which cut one's fingers to
pieces, and generally came out by the roots.
With the proverbial luck of the first day, I got
a shot, but of course missed, which, under the
circumstances, was not surprising, having to lean
the most of my precious body over a precipice
and fire straight down on to the back of an ibex
perched on a rock 150 yards below me, while
Rama held on to my heels like grim death. To
feel myself safe once more in my tent was a very
considerable satisfaction, while I intimated gently
to Rama that ibex-shooting was not my style of
business. "Oh," he replied, "all sahibs are the
same; but after a day or two they become too
foolhardy, and it is all I can do to prevent them
from breaking their necks. We will shoot a bear
or two first: the ground is not so difficult, for
they come down into the nullahs to feed, and in
a few days we will try the ibex-ground again."
Well, we shot some red bears, and found it very
easy work; for poor old Bruin cannot see, and

therefore requires no stalking, and very little climbing. Meanwhile I had discovered what a wonderful thing a grass-shoe[1] is, and when on the third day we returned to the ibex-ground, I felt as safe as a goat.

After a blank morning, we sat down to eat the breakfast we had brought up the mountain, and as we rested the *chota*, or small shikari, who had been prospecting, came hurrying up to report a herd of ibex. Off we went over the snow, and soon came upon the herd lying in a large corrie. At first I thought them unstalkable; but as the ground was well covered with rocks, I soon found myself near enough for a shot. " Oh, sahib, do not be in a hurry," was Rama's advice; "your hand is shaking: the ibex are all lying down, and will not run away." Certainly it was a word in season, for I was in a great state of what they call in the Highlands "stag-fever." So I lay quiet until one got up: of course he looked to me the "biggest as ever was." I could resist no longer, and loosed off at him; in an instant he and the rest had vanished!

---

[1] The so-called grass-shoe is a sandal woven of a rope made of rice-straw, and worn over a moccasin made of leather or thick cloth.

"*Lugga*, sahib, you have hit him."

Away we went as hard as we could over the brow of the hill, and there, oh joy! was my ibex, and down too. "Wait, sahib, wait," was the warning cry. I could not, but ran on towards him, when to my horror up he got; bang went the second barrel, and missed! The agony of that moment, and the relief when he dropped never to rise again! Having, as I considered, earned a rest, I proceeded back to Srinagar.

My bag consisted now of one ibex (36-inch horns), two musk-deer, and three bears. After a week at Srinagar, I began to think this was not much to swagger about; so consulted Rama, and was soon on the way back to the Wardwan, where, finding that a man had just vacated the Crushnai valley, quite the best nullah in the Wardwan district, I popped in, and in a month shot half-a-dozen ibex, and left a confirmed hill-shooter: loafing in the Kashmir valley had now no charm for me.

My next expedition was to Pangi, where I was first in the field, crossing over the Chini Pass—now forbidden as dangerous—and secured the Sechu nullah, since reserved by the Rajah of Chumba. There fortune favoured me, getting in twenty-five days' shooting twenty-five head—viz., ten ibex, eight bears, and seven musk-deer.

From there I wandered on to Zanskar, and tried for burrel, but saw no heads worth shooting, so proceeded to Leh, where, after resting a while with friends, I again prepared for a start, having in my mind to add yak, burrel, Tibet antelope, and a possible *Ovis Ammon* to my collection.

After a twelve-days' march we reached the Kobrang valley, where traces of yak were soon found, and, what was more to the purpose, shot a couple, one of them a very fine bull. The rest of the herd would not go, and I might have killed them all had I wished to do so, as they ran round and round me.

Then moving back to Kiam in Changchenmo, I shot a couple of antelopes, but found them very difficult to stalk, as they live on the open grass plain. Continuing my way over the Marsemik Pass, I came across a herd of burrel, one of which I shot; then had two days' of unsuccessful hunting after a herd of *Ovis Ammon*, which frequent this range. This brought my expedition to an end, and I returned to Kashmir. Latterly I used a single Henry 500-bore in place of the old muzzle-loader with which I began, and found it quite the best weapon for mountain-shooting. A double barrel, take it all round, is a dangerous weapon, especially for a beginner, as he is pretty sure to fire his left too soon after his first shot at a retreating animal, which is perhaps a small head not worth shooting, and if he hits it, which is doubtful, will not kill it clean; whereas the short time it takes to reload gives the chance of a steady shot during the short pause which a herd generally makes after the first spurt, very often on the sky-line, when they turn to see the cause of the disturbance before finally separating. Then, if you have had patience, is the time to select a good head with a fair chance of killing. Or, if moving on bad ground where they travel slowly, you can get three or more shots.

My chief object in life after this was to get markhor. So, as my amiable commanding officer sent my name in for another spell of leave, I proceeded once more to Kashmir.

By the advice of a friend I got Kamala, one of the best shikaris, and started up the Rupel valley, west of Nanga Parbat, with the intention of going over into Chilas. This, Kamala said, was somewhat risky, as Chilas was *yagistan*— literally, a lawless place; but if I promised to avoid villages, and keep on high ground, it was possible we might get a markhor, and return without our throats being cut!

Going to the foot of the Rupel glacier, I left my camp standing, and taking half-a-dozen coolies with necessaries, started to find my way over the pass. This I did without much trouble, except from my coolies, who kept collapsing, saying they were dying, and could go no farther. However, I got over at last, and curled up below the glacier for the night.

The next morning, making an early start, we caught sight of some natives, and as neither appeared to be very confident of the other, we had a talk across the ravine! After explaining I only wanted a markhor, two of them started off for the Malik (headman), while we agreed to remain there for him. In a couple of hours he appeared, and inviting me over to confer with him, we soon became quite friendly. Grey-bearded and venerable in appearance, he reminded me of the patriarchs of old, and very kindly offered me a hut, and a man to show me the ground, the only proviso being that I should make but a short stay, for fear some other Malik might hear of me, and take a fancy to my goods and chattels. I thanked him much, and offered him a snuff-box, which sealed our bond of friendship, then started for his little summer residence, which consisted of a few mud-huts.

Next day the guide came early, and off we went. I was delighted with the look of the country, and felt confident if markhor were about we should see them: being above the forest region, there was nothing to hide them. We saw none until the afternoon, when, to my great joy, I discovered a splendid herd. All seemed to be old heads, with magnificent neck-manes and beards. I made a good stalk, and knocked over three, one of which, however, got away, being only stunned, I fancy, with a knock on the horn, as there was no blood-track. The two remaining were good ones, resembling the Kajinag heads as to twist, and were not in the least like the Astor heads.

The following day I devoted to skinning and cleaning these specimens. Then the old Malik came and said, "You have got what you wished. Now take my advice and return, or the Malik of Booner may find you out, and I cannot protect you." At first I was disinclined to believe this, but Kamala and the coolies begged me with tears to go; so I agreed, and started immediately. Afterwards I heard from Biddulph, who was then Resident at Astor, that the other man did turn up, and rather sat on my old Malik for befriending me.

CHAPTER II.

SPORTING WANDERINGS.

THE PILGRIM AT THE BRIDGE—SHOOTING BURREL—IN THE PIR PANJAL AFTER MARKHOR—A NARROW ESCAPE—DEATH OF RASAKA—RETURN TO LEH—FESTIVAL AT A *GOMPA*—ACROSS THE SASAR AND KARAKORAM PASSES—AN OASIS—*OVIS AMMON* AND SHAPOO.

AFTER a good deal of travelling and *contretemps* of various kinds, without any particular sport, I made up my mind to have a look at Colonel Markham's old shooting-ground above Gangootri, of which I had read an account when he went there years ago with shikari Wilson.

The road as far as the Hindoo shrine was quite good, but after that I found it rather difficult. There being no bridges, I had to cut down trees and make them myself. After a few days' hard work I got up to the Gaomukhi, or Cow's Mouth, as the natives call the mouth of the glacier. It was a lovely camping-ground, commanding a view of one of the finest glaciers in the world, with a glorious amphitheatre of mountains covered with everlasting snow.

I was accompanied to this spot by one of the numerous pilgrims who flock up every year to worship at the shrine of Gangajee, having found the poor creature squatting down in his yellow cloth by the side of a little swinging bridge of wire which crosses the gorge through which the Bilung river, a tributary of the Ganges, flows. Except to a mountaineer, walking across is rather jumpy work, as it is only one plank wide, swung on wire, and sways a good deal. If you look down to the torrent rushing and foaming 500 feet below, it is by no means conducive to steady nerves.

In reply to my query as to why he had not crossed, the unfortunate pilgrim told me that he had been there for two days and had started time after time, but always failed for lack of nerve. I then asked if he would trust me to take him across, and he said he would, "for the sahibs never failed in their promises." So telling him to take hold of my belt, shut his eyes, and follow, he did so like a lamb, and in a couple of minutes we were at the other side. I looked round and told him to open his eyes and let go. Never did I see a man look so happy; he fell down and embraced my knees. He followed me to Gaomukhi, staying near my tent all the time I was there. He used to say his prayers at the mouth of the glacier, and meditate in his yellow cloth for the rest of his time. I could not get him to eat anything but a little rice and dall, although burrel-meat was plentiful in my camp. He only asked for the skin of a beast to take back with him as a souvenir.

I shot burrel in this spot until I was ashamed, and left, taking seventeen heads with me. I marched down the Bhagarutti as far as Batwari, then took a line across the hills to British Gurwal *viâ* Okimat and Pomwali.

At one camp I heard a good many sambur trumpeting at night, so took a look round the forest next day, and came across one or two beautiful stags, quite the finest horns I ever saw; but as they were in velvet, did not shoot them, only wished much it had been a month later.

After this I made my way back to Dagshai, where my regiment was then stationed.

My next four months' leave I decided to try for markhor in the Pir Panjal, and met old Sadik, a shikari who had lived there all his life, and knew every markhor by name. For three weeks we worked in the Bakri and Andar nullahs, but only saw small heads, so went off to Kashmir.

I got Rasaka, a shikari I had known formerly, and started for the Wardwan, having promised to get some ibex for the mess. All the good nullahs were taken; but on my way I happened to meet the occupant of Crushnai, in the Wardwan district, who had come as far as the Margan pass to meet his wife. This he offered to me, as he had soon to leave, promising to let me know when he did so. Meanwhile I went into the Mangal nullah, where I had not only great grief, but a narrow escape for my life.

As we went out in the morning, Rasaka told me how two sportsmen and their followers had been killed in this nullah, showing me the place where the snow came on them. I remarked that I had little experience of avalanches, but was more afraid of the rocks when they came down with a run. Now and again in our lives a casual remark seems prophetic, and it proved to be so on this occasion.

We were working our way down a very steep snow-filled rift on the mountain-side, a coolie from the nearest village leading, Rasaka next, and I last of all. We were moving in *échelon*, and had only got a few hundred yards down, when I was startled by a whizz on the snow: before I could look round or say a word, a flattish rock the size of a cart-wheel went past me like a toboggan, caught poor Rasaka behind the knees, turned him over, and sent him spinning down the snow on to the coolie in front, and the two went off head over heels. I felt very sick, thinking they would never stop until they went over the *kud* at the bottom of the ravine; but, to my great relief, they came against the side of the rift, which took a bend some way below, and there they hung on. I got down to Rasaka first, and for the moment thought he was not much hurt; but when I asked him, he replied quite quietly, "Sahib, I am done for; look at my leg." And, sure enough, it was smashed all to pieces — almost knocked off! I ran on to the other man, who was groaning; but finding he was all right beyond a bruise or two, shook him up, telling him it was no time for crying, and we must see what could be done for Rasaka. Finding it was impossible to move him any distance, I decided there was nothing for it but to return to camp and rig up some sort of a litter to carry him down in; but as I doubted much getting back before dark, when travelling on such bad ground would be dangerous, we moved him into a sort of cave, where, making him as comfortable as was possible under the circumstances, I left him with the coolie, telling him if I did not return in time he must stay there for the night. I had some difficulty in finding my way without a guide, and did not get down before dark. Early next morning I was back, and got the poor fellow down to the village, which was not far from my camp. He then told me he felt certain he should not live for twenty-four hours; and as he was spitting and passing blood, I feared it was too likely. He died that night. I was much distressed at losing him like this, and was very glad to get a note from a friend asking me to join him, so left the fatal spot at once. I stayed in Crushnai a month, killed a dozen ibex, and so kept my promise to the mess.

During my next leave, in 1884, I determined to go as far as I could towards Chinese Turkistan on the Yarkand road. I reached Leh, where I found an old friend, Fraser by name, who was Joint Commissioner, and with his kind assistance soon made arrangements for a start. But as the Sasar and Khardung passes were not quite open, I went up with him to Hemmis to see a great festival at the *gompa* or monastery there. It was curious, but rather monotonous. The court of the *gompa* was decorated with flags and pictures, and the lamas performed many quaint dances in masks and fancy dresses. I went over the establishment, and found it quite like the European monastery, with refectory, library, and cells; also that the lamas, like the monks of old, took very good care of the inner man! The head lama wears a red cardinal's hat on state occasions.

Having got my caravan in order, I started off over the Digar La, which is a fairly easy pass, and found myself on the Yarkand road. After crossing the Shyok river in a boat, the ponies swimming, I proceeded up the Nubra valley for two days. Here I bade adieu to the habitations of man and crossed over the Sasar Pass. It was hard work for the ponies, the winding path being covered with *débris* and moraines of glaciers all the way, until reaching the glacier itself. Over this the going was good enough, as the snow on the top was caked hard. But the descent on the other side was just the reverse, and our difficulties were great. However, getting over at last, I camped on the shore of the Shyok river.

The next morning, crossing the river with my tent, &c., in the ferry-boat, the ponies swimming as before, I loaded on the other side, and proceeded up a narrow gorge to the plains of Murghi. It was early morning, and the water in the stream, which I forded about fifty times, was low, so had little trouble and made a good march. The following day I crossed the Depsang plains, 17,000 feet above the level of the sea, and found myself again on the Shyok river, now a very shallow stream.

My next obstacle was the Karakoram, 18,500 feet; but it was easy going, and I did not feel it in the least.

Two days after, I reached Wahab Jilga, from which it was my intention to go over a pass called Karatagh towards Kizil Jilga, where yak are said to swarm. Failing, however, to strike the road, I found myself, after two days' travelling, at the top of the Potash gorge, which leads down to the Karakash river. It was a pleasant sight for "sair een," the beautiful green grass, rose-bushes, tamarisk, and wild-flowers, after the eternal gravel, dust, and shale of the road. My ponies, too, evidently relished the change when they got their packs off and were given the run of their teeth.

I stayed there three days to rest and feed them, and then started back, having promised not to cross the river into Chinese territory for fear of political complications, intending to try once more to find the road to Kizil Jilga; but finding I could not shake off an attack of fever which developed the day I arrived at Potash, decided to return to Leh, and had a most unpleasant journey, fever every two days. As soon, however, as I got into Nubra and had apricots and vegetables, I picked up quickly, and had quite recovered by the time I reached Leh.

Having only shot a couple of antelopes this trip, I pushed on to Gya, hoping for an *Ovis Ammon*, and in three marches reached the Kamer nullah, though by no means sanguine of the result, knowing others had been there already. However, on the evening of the third day I got my chance, killing two: one good head went off with what I took to be a shapoo with him, the rest of the herd taking another direction. Getting back to camp late, I found Colonel Thornton, who was envious of my luck, having had no shot. As I had to leave next day, having promised to meet Fraser at Miroo, I recommended him to hunt for the *Ovis* that had gone off with the shapoo.

Starting early next morning, and crossing over the ridge of the Kamer on my way into the Miroo nullah, I came on the very *Ovis* and shapoo of the previous day, made an easy stalk, and shot them both. The shapoo proved to be a hybrid *Ovis;* the *Ovis* was a very fine one, but the horns a good deal broken. I hesitated about letting Colonel Thornton know, but on second thoughts deemed it better not to destroy his hopes. I did no more shooting, being again troubled with fever, so returned with a couple of friends to Kashmir.

CHAPTER III.

START FOR CHINESE TURKISTAN.

PREPARATIONS FOR TRIP TO CHINESE TURKISTAN AND PAMIRS—PROCURE A GUIDE—START WITH CAPTAIN BOWER BY THE SCIND VALLEY—BAGGAGE PONY DROWNED—GOVERNMENT INTERFERES—M. DAUVERGNE JOINS US—CLIMBING THE KHARDUNG PASS—THE SPOT WHERE DALGLEISH WAS MURDERED—A COURT OF INQUIRY.

BEING now a free man, having completed twenty years' service and sent in my papers, time was no longer a matter of consideration. I therefore began my preparations for the trip so long thought of, to the new dominion of Chinese Turkistan, having previously applied for a passport, about which there was considerable difficulty.

The Foreign Office handed the application over to the India Office, the India Office to the Foreign Office in India. Finally, the Foreign Office in India said the Foreign Office in England must procure it from Pekin; but at length I received it, and was at liberty to proceed. I had arranged with Captain Bower of the 17th Bengal Cavalry to accompany me, for which he procured a year's leave from June 1889.

This business completed, I employed my spare days trying for markhor (*Capra megaceros*) on my way in to Kashmir on the Pir Panjal range, but saw none worth a shot. I got, however, three tahr (*Hemitragus jemlaicus*) and a couple of bears. The former I was very glad to have, requiring a specimen to complete my Indian collection.

On May 9th I got to Srinagar and began making preparations for a start. My great idea was to get to the Pamirs without going to Yarkand, as I feared the Chinese authorities would hinder me as much as they could from going anywhere off the main road, and determined therefore, if possible, to leave the Yarkand road at Aktagh and take a course north-west through Raskum to Sarikol. As this route had never been explored by an Englishman, I thought it would suit Bower well, he having been granted leave on the understanding that he should do some mapping.

The first proceeding was to arrange for a team of ponies and a guide. By good luck an old friend of mine, a Ladaki, who held an appointment of some importance at Leh, happened to be in Srinagar—having brought down a party of lamas to perform with their band before General (now Lord) Roberts, the Commander-in-Chief, who was on a visit to the Maharajah. As he had a good deal to do with the people who frequent the road between Yarkand and Leh,—merchants, &c., who provide ponies for caravans, called *karakash*,—he was the very one to help us, and procured the most suitable man for the business. Baratbai was his name, and he happened to know Sirikul and the Southern Pamirs well, having been there more than once getting poli-horns from the Kirghiz to sell in India. He had just come down with a consignment, and said he would be delighted to go with us, and knew the Raskum road, but that it was too early to start, the rivers being too high, and the fords, of which there were many, too deep, so that it was useless to leave Leh until the middle of August. All I wanted was to get my polis before winter set in; therefore I arranged with him to supply as many ponies as required, that we should start from Leh as soon as the road was open, proceed *viâ* Raskum along the foot of the Mustagh range on to the Sarikol Pamir, there to hunt as long as I wished, and then, if I pleased, to go to the Little and Great Pamir, and on to Yarkand,—the trip to occupy any length of time up to four months, for which I agreed to pay him 100 rupees for each baggage-pony, he to find drivers and spare ponies to carry grain, and feed them all. This was all put upon stamped paper in due form, with 300 rupees in advance to enable him to make his arrangements.

There was nothing further to do but lay in stores and *toshkarna*—*i.e.*, pieces of cloth, *lungis*, *king-kob*, a few watches, and odds and ends, for presents to the inhabitants of the country we were to visit. This system of exchanging presents in the East is a great nuisance, and costs a good deal of money.

Everything was now in order. My battery consisted of a double express of Dougal's which had done me very good service for fifteen years, a smooth-bore gun, and last, and least in size but not in importance, a Martini-Henry carbine. I got this from the arsenal at Ferozepore, and sighted it myself to shoot four drams of powder with an express bullet, making it shoot beautifully at 150 yards. This weapon it was my intention to have always with me, and carried it on a bucket slung on a native cavalry-saddle, the thing of all others for that kind of work, as it carries all sorts of odds and ends, and if carefully adjusted never gives a sore back, besides being comfortable for a long day's march. When in full marching order I filled it up in the following manner: Behind the cantel I slung my carbine in bucket on one side, my soldier's canteen for food purposes in a leather case on the near side; on the D.'s behind the cantel was rolled a good big Inverness cape made of thick *puttoo* (Kashmir homespun), and in front a pair of wallets for anything else. This arrangement I found most convenient, and never altered it during the whole trip.

On June 17th Bower arrived, and on the 22d we bade adieu to our kind friends in Srinagar, and started for Gandarbal, at the mouth of the Sind valley. We were accompanied by Major Johnstone Douglas[1] of the 5th Lancers, who intended to march to Simla *viâ* Leh.

[1] The sad news of Major Johnstone Douglas's death at Simla has reached me since writing the above.

Our first stage in the Sind valley was Kangan: it is a pretty road, and all went well. On our next day's march to Revel, however, we had a terrible mishap. The road here and there follows the banks of the Sind river, which at this season is a mighty torrent. At Gond we sat down and waited for our traps to come up, that we might breakfast. After a short time one of our servants arrived looking utterly flabbergasted. He told us that the ponies had got jammed in turning a corner where the roadway was cut out on the banks of the river, and one of them was hustled over the edge into the stream: having a heavy load, he disappeared at once, and was never seen again.

The man was in such a state of mind that we had some difficulty in discovering what the load was; but when everything had turned up, we found that, besides other important articles, it consisted of Johnstone Douglas's battery, a double express, and one of Holland's paradox guns, which he set great store by. I never was so grieved for any one in my life. Here he was without a weapon of any sort, going a long journey through a shooting country. He took it wonderfully well, saying it was the fortune of war. I was especially sorry, feeling in a measure responsible, having persuaded him to come. He sent back word to the authorities in Kashmir, but with very little hope of seeing his things again.

On July 7th we reached Leh, after a very hot march up the Indus valley. Our dogs suffered much, and poor Johnstone Douglas had another blow in the loss of his favourite fox-terrier. Karakash Baratbai was there before us, and said he was feeding up his ponies, but that we must wait another month, as there was no chance of crossing the rivers for some time. We also found Dauvergne, a Frenchman, there, who had long been settled in Kashmir, and had travelled a great deal, and who intended taking the same road as ourselves. He had brought up a stone pillar which he intended to set up on the spot where poor Dalgleish was murdered the year before by Dad Mahomed, a Pathan. Douglas and I were just starting off for Gya with the intention of trying for an *Ovis Ammon*, when Captain Ramsay, who is Joint-Commissioner at Leh, came over to our bungalow and said information had been received of our intention to travel to the Pamir *viâ* Ruskum, and that by order of the

Government of India we were not to be allowed to start until we had signed certificates to the effect that we would not leave the main road until we had crossed the Kilian Pass into Chinese Turkistan. This took me quite aback, having taken good care not to mention it to any but those immediately concerned, fearing something of the sort would happen. The reason given by the Government of India was that they did not consider the road safe on account of the marauding Kunjuts who infest it. We were much disappointed, but there was no help for it, so we signed the agreement.

Under these circumstances, the sooner we were off the better, as we should have to make rather a long *détour*. Our intention now was to leave the main road as soon as we had crossed the Kilian: we should then be on the Chinese border, and the matter would rest between us and the Chinese. Baratbai told us he had heard of a path which branched off towards Kugiar due west from the main road. As it was unexplored, and would probably take us to Sirikul quicker than going to Yarkand and back to Sirikul, we determined to try it. This also suited Dauvergne, whose object was to shoot some poli on the

Taghdumbash, and return to Kashmir by Chitral and Gilghit in early winter.

Having laid in a stock of cotton goods, consisting of *chogas, lungis*, prints, muslin, and coloured handkerchiefs, to exchange with the natives for sheep, milk, butter, &c., we started on July 27, very glad to be off at last. We sent the kit on early, and at 2 P.M. ordered our ponies to be saddled. This we found easier said than done. Our animals were of the Kalmuk breed, who possess a great deal of character, and that not of the best. They objected most strongly to the proceeding, no doubt knowing by hard and bitter experience what a sore back was like, and preferring to eat green lucerne in orchards in Ladak to living on two tea-cups of barley per diem, varied with what *burtsa* they could pick up on the road. After blindfolding, twitching, tying up legs, and all sorts of dodges, we succeeded in getting into the saddle, and bade adieu to our kind friend the Commissioner.

We found our camp already pitched at the foot of the Khardung, at an altitude of 16,000 feet, and very considerably colder than at Leh. At break of day we began to climb the pass, which resembles many others in the far Himalayas, being a gradual ascent up a great barren corrie, until within a couple of thousand feet of the crest, when the road becomes more abrupt and zigzags to the top. Our ponies seemed to feel the altitude very much, though unladen, having put our things on yaks for the first two marches. Just over the col, on the northern side, there is a nasty bit of frozen snow and ice which has been the death of many a good pony. The Wazir had been so good as to send a gang of men there to cut a foothold in the ice, so that by passing them on carefully, one man hanging on by the head and another to the tail of each pony when he got to a bad place, we got them safely over the dangerous parts. From there a small glacier runs down to a tarn about a mile from the crest, and the road continues down the corrie. After about five miles we debouched into the Shyok valley. There we unloaded our ponies at the ferry. Owing to there being only one boat, and the stream running very strong, it was nearly evening when we got all our kit across. Continuing our march, we reached Salti, and camped on a nice plot, with grazing handy for the ponies.

Our breakfast was taken in an orchard next

day, where the apricots kept tumbling down asking to be eaten. At Taghar we camped in one similar. These oases, for you can call them nothing else, are numerous in the Nubra valley, which is very well cultivated, the people making good use of their short summer; and besides such fruit as apples and apricots, the land produces good crops of grain, bearded wheat and barley, and lucerne-grass: the latter is much affected by the Yarkandi caravan-ponies when they come in from their starvation journey from Turkistan. The only drawback to camping in these charming little orchards is that, unless you are very careful in taking precautions, there is always a chance of having your tent and kit swamped, as the streams which irrigate them come from the hills above, and being fed by snow, always increase towards evening.

At Panamikh we determined to halt for a day to give our ponies a final good feed, and lay in our stock of grain and flour,—this being the last village where supplies can be procured on the Yarkand road, and nothing can be got in the way of grain until Shahidula, a sort of halfway house, where a certain Pathan called Ian Mahomed sets up his camp in the caravan season, and supplies traders at rather an exorbitant rate.

From Changlang we crossed the Carawul Pass to Totiyalek. The road was very rough and stony, winding amongst *débris* of granite and shale. Our ponies were not in until late; but having gone a good way towards the Sasar Pass, it left less climbing for the morrow. This was our first really cold camp, being amongst glaciers.

The road over the Sasar Pass is a very bad one, winding over the moraines of glaciers, which come down each side of the gorge. It was a good scramble to the top, where there was fresh snow, but not enough to impede us much. Once over, we again camped on the Shyok.

Nothing eventful happened before reaching Shahidula, except the destruction of a Tibet antelope by Bower at Wahab Jilga.

We found the Karakoram very easy, with no snow. On reaching the spot where Dalgleish was murdered, we found the stone pillar which had been sent on ahead by Dauvergne. There he set it up. I only wish we could have put the head of Dad Mahomed on a post on the other side.

After halting four days to rest the ponies, we

left Shahidula for Sanju Kurgaon. We had rather a disturbed night at the ford owing to rain and storm. Dauvergne's tent was nearly knocked over by a stray pony, who imagined he could get in by the back-door, and tried to do so, thinking, no doubt, it was more comfortable to be inside than out. Caravan-ponies have a great fancy for pottering about tents, and stumbling over the ropes.

At Sanju Kurgaon there is an old frontier fort, now in ruins. Here the Kilian and Sanju roads bifurcate. The Sanju road was formerly open to caravans; but the Chinese, for some reason of their own, have closed it, which is a pity, being by all accounts a better road than the Kilian.

As we continued our way the road grew very steep, winding up the side of the gorge towards the Kilian Pass, the ponies going slowly, being very short of wind. Our camping-ground on the side of the mountain was very indifferent, and we had to keep the ponies tied head and tail all night to prevent them wandering back the way they came.

The pass itself was very easy,—no snow to speak of, although over 17,000 feet. Descending the gorge for ten miles, we came on a nice bit of grass with one or two Kirghiz *yurts*[1] on it, and made our camp for the night. Here we had our first trouble with Baratbai. Three of his drivers came and said they must leave him, as he had the temper of the devil, but that they wanted their pay before starting. They had been engaged, they said, to go with him by the Yarkand road, and now they were being taken they knew not where. I was much exercised at the prospect of losing half my drivers, and told them wherever we went I would answer for it they should not be losers. They still insisted, though Baratbai said they were not entitled to anything, being paid in advance. When I told him he must pay them extra to keep them, he said it was as much as his life was worth after the row they had had, as they were Pathans, and would cut his throat the first opportunity. So I called a court of inquiry, with Dogpa (Dauvergne's servant) as president, to try and settle the matter. After a stormy meeting, it was agreed that Baratbai should pay something, and that on arrival at Yarkand the affair should be settled by the Aksakal, or magistrate. The three men were then told they might go.

[1] A *yurt* is a dome-shaped tent made of felt.

We went about fourteen miles down the valley to where a tributary nullah joined from the north-west. This, we concluded, from information given us by the Kirghiz at the last camp, was the spot where we should leave the main road; so we sat down and waited for the caravan. Baratbai soon came up, said we were right, and that, though he had never been by the road, he had a general idea of it. He knew we could get to Kugiar this way, and after that he knew all the roads in the Sirikul well, having been born and bred there. This latter I found to be a very respectable lie, for he was born a Kunjuti, and sold as a slave to a Sirikuli by his parents when they were hard up! Two miles up this valley was a fair bit of grass for the ponies, so we camped there.

In this country the three necessaries of camp-life are generally found together — viz., grass, water, and fuel; for unless there is a stream or spring there is no grass, and where there is grass ponies or yaks have left their traces in the way of dung, which soon dries and furnishes fuel. This, together with *burtsa*—a sort of wild lavender or wormwood plant with a woodeny root, which contains a certain amount of oil, and burns freely even when green—is the fuel generally found on the Pamirs and plains of Central Asia.

We had now left the beaten track of Yarkand, and were getting into a country as yet unexplored by Europeans. Bower produced his prismatic compass, and began plotting from where our new road turned off.

CHAPTER IV.

JOURNEY TO THE PAMIRS.

HOSPITALITY OF THE WAKHIS—A STIFF CLIMB—AN UNEXPECTED FRIEND—THE RUSSIAN'S CAMP—PLAINS OF TURKISTAN—DISTINGUISHED VISITORS—WE LOSE OUR WAY—A FERTILE VALLEY—THE BEG OF KARGALIK—A SUCCESSFUL DEAL—CROSSING THE YARKAND RIVER—A NOVEL RAFT-PROPELLER—THE HAKIM BEG AWAITS OUR ARRIVAL—A STATE VISIT—AN AWKWARD FALL—FIRST SIGNS OF *OVIS POLI*—MORE INTERVIEWS—THE TAGHDUMBASH PAMIR—A WOLF IN THE WAY—CHANGING GROUND.

PROCEEDING up the same nullah, we came to a camp of Wakhis, or people of Wakhan, a tract of country lying north of Kunjut. Like the Kirghiz, they are nomads, but totally different from them in feature, physique, and character,—altogether a much superior race. Several of them had come over from Wakhan and settled in this country, paying tribute to the Chinese, and are, in fact, naturalised Chinese subjects. Their hospitality delayed us a little, for they brought out bowls of butter-milk and bread, which our servants were nothing loath to accept. They told us our road left the valley and wound over a spur called the Kisnach Loch Dawan.[1] It was steep, but otherwise good enough, and by mid-day we reached the top, Bower taking the altitude at 14,000 feet. We were rather disappointed not getting a view from the ridge, which was blocked by another spur running parallel to the one we stood on.

A similar march the following day brought us to another Wakhi camp at the foot of the Saragat Pass, 14,000 feet. Here the same ceremony of refreshment occurred, and one of the natives offered to come on with us as far as the next camping-ground as guide, for which we were very thankful, for no one in the caravan had an idea of the way. It was a much stiffer climb than the previous day, and this our ponies soon found out, requiring much driving. All things have an end, however, and we got over at last, and slithered down the other side. From what the Wakhis told us, we found that until we got to Kugiar every march would be very much alike, with a *topa dawan* (pass of earth) to cross, until we struck the Tisnaf river.

[1] *Dawan* is the Turki for *pass*.

The spurs we were crossing seemed very similar in height and formation, and appeared to run north and east from the Mustagh, merging into a subsidiary range of hills running parallel to the said Mustagh—in fact, much alike in formation to the Sewaliks at the foot of the Himalayas, only much higher.

I had questioned our guide about the game in the neighbourhood. There were, he said, ibex and burrel in abundance on the hills in the winter, but at this time of year (August) they moved off to the higher ranges, as the sheep, goats, and yak were all over the place. Chikore, marmots, and hares we saw numbers of, also snow-cock at the higher altitudes.

The Tusla Dawan was a much harder ascent, and we had terrible work to get our ponies over: one, White Surrey by name, went down, and it was with the greatest difficulty we got him on his legs again, he was so utterly done, though to look at he was one of the best. Some of the others showed signs of striking work, so we loaded our riding-ponies, who had had an easy time of it, as we had walked nearly all the way, and managed to get over at last; but Bower and I came to the conclusion that unless we could get a team of yaks, and so give the ponies a rest, we should never get to Sirikul. By good luck we saw some grazing near our next camp, and arranged with the Malik (headman) for a team of ten. This was a great relief to our minds; for to break down where we were would have been wretched indeed, while four days without a load, and a fair amount of grass, which they said we should find, would pull the cripples round wonderfully.

The yaks were so late in coming that we began to be afraid our friends had repented of their bargain; but at ten o'clock they appeared, saying they had some trouble in catching them, for, when grazing, *Bos gruniens* becomes rather wild. It was useless attempting to cross the Topa Dawan that day; so, coming to a good ground, we determined to unload and give the beasts a chance of a mouthful of grass. This was certainly the best ground of the whole journey. On the banks of a river, which looked as if it ought to be full of fish, extended a broad strip of grass, with groves of willow and birch-trees, and here and there patches of tamarisk jungle. The grass was very good, and our ponies thoroughly enjoyed themselves. Not so the poor yaks, however; for their drivers said if they were loosed for a moment they would be off to their last camp, and so, like Tantalus, they were tied up with food under their noses, of which they could not partake.

A long but gradual ascent took us up the Dawan-Urtang, 15,000 feet. The view from the top was the same as usual—everlasting parallel ridges. Descending about the same distance, we camped on turf. I was rather exercised, when the caravan came in, to find that Jaffer, our interpreter and general servant, the most useful man we had, had been taken ill. He came up soon after, riding one of the ponies, looking very sick. I promised him a pill or two, which gave him some comfort, and he said that no doubt my all-powerful medicine would soon put him right.

Again we crossed a pass of 15,000 feet, then wound our way by a stony ravine, the sides rising in precipitous cliffs, very nearly meeting overhead in places. At about 3 P.M. we began to look out for a camping-ground; but as the stream which we had followed for some time had disappeared underground, there was nothing for it but to follow on until it vouchsafed to reappear. The valley gradually opened out; several branch nullahs joined it, but still no water. At last we came to a beautiful bit of grass-land, in the middle of which we saw some *yurts*, and so concluded that the long-expected stream had come to light again. A native soon appeared, and to my astonishment addressed me in Hindostani. He said he was very pleased to see a sahib again; that all he had was mine; and that the *sahib log* were the most wonderful people in the world. I asked him what he was, and how he came to be settled in this out-of-the-way place. He replied he was a Kashmiri, and was in Turkistan in the time of Yakub Beg; that when the Chinese conquered the country, and were killing right and left, he ran off with a few sheep and goats by the Kugiar road, and so came to where I found him, and was well satisfied to remain, there being water and grass for his sheep, of which he had now a good many, and had managed to raise enough Indian corn to keep his family. On hearing we were going to Ak Masjid next day, he mentioned there was a party of Russians camped there with many Cossacks and camels. The object of their visit was, however, unknown to him.

The stream we had followed joined the Tiznaf

river; but it was impossible to follow it at this season, owing to the banks being overflown and the fords very deep and rapid. Accordingly we retraced our steps a mile and a half, and crossed over the Kitchikul Pass, 16,000 feet. It was a good pull; but the yaks did their work nobly, and we got up all right. We then followed a narrow ravine downwards for six miles, when water began to trickle through the gravel, and soon after came to a *yurt*. We went on, fully expecting to come to some sort of town or village: nothing greeted our eyes but groups of *yurts* at intervals, until the water disappeared, and with it the *yurts*. We had a talk with the Beg, or headman, who told us this was Ak Masjid, and that about two miles lower the Russians were encamped, but that there was no water, and they sent camels up frequently with water-skins to fetch it. Soon after, we came on a string of them escorted by Cossacks, evidently being brought back from grazing: they looked in very poor condition. Going on far enough to be clear of the dogs, who made night hideous near the *yurts*, Bower and I camped. Dauvergne said he would join the Russians. As soon as we had had a wash and changed, we went in search of their camp, which we found about a mile and a half down the nullah. It consisted of two or three big *yurts*, and some long sort of pall tents for the Cossacks. Dogpa (Dauvergne's servant) showed the *yurt* of the commanding officer of the expedition, Colonel Pieutrow, who, with three other officers and twenty-five Cossacks, was carrying on General Prejvalski's explorations towards Tibet. They had been camped there some time feeding up the camels, which they had brought with them from Russian Turkistan, and when ready intended to proceed *via* Khotan towards Polo.

The colonel was very civil, and taking us into the mess-*yurt*, which was very comfortable, we squatted down on the *mundas* (felt carpet) and partook of the conventional glass of tea and a cigar. He and one other officer spoke French, so we got on all right. They asked us to stay and sup with them; but we excused ourselves, being some distance from our camp, and having had a pretty hard day of it. In course of conversation it transpired that they had crossed the Tian Shan mountains by the Bedal Pass, and proceeded *via* Ushturfan to the Zarafshan river, which they struck somewhere about Tumchuk, and then followed the river-bank to Yarkand.

Going down early, we found Dauvergne ready for a start, so, bidding our friends good-bye, we proceeded on our road, following the same nullah as before. As we advanced it opened out, and the hills becoming lower on each side, showed that we were approaching the plains of Turkistan. Here we had our first experience of the mists of that country, which are frequent during summer. The sun was completely veiled, and for this we were not sorry, as we should otherwise have had a hot march. There was no water, except here and there a stagnant pool, which was so nasty that the ponies even would not touch it, though they had none before starting. Turning a corner, we saw what appeared to be a tower looming in the distance; but on approaching nearer, this proved to be a large poplar-tree, which meant water, and also the end of our day's march, for which we were not sorry, and, distinguishing a grove of poplars and willows with a few huts, like the camel of the desert we quickened our pace, and soon reached the long-wished-for oasis.

At first the little village appeared to be deserted, but after poking about we found a native Turki, who told us we were about six miles from Kugiar, the first place of importance on the Turkistan plain. Here, he said, was a Chinese *karaol*, or frontier post, but that we had better camp where we were, and that he would supply us with fuel, eggs, milk, and fowls, and our ponies would find lots of grazing on the edge of the little canal which irrigated the few fields which surrounded the village. This canal, on exploration, we found started from a spring at the foot of the poplar we had first sighted.

The mist was thicker than ever, so we could get no view of the country ahead—rather a disappointment, for after travelling so long amongst high mountains, a view of a plain is always a pleasant change to the eye, even if it be a desert, as by all accounts this was.

We pitched our camp in a little grove of apricot-trees, and in a short time our friend from the village turned up with the promised supplies, —the eggs and fowls being especially welcome after the hard fare on which we had been for the last month. We determined to halt the next day, for as we had travelled from Shahidula without a pause, we considered that both ourselves and our beasts were entitled to the rest.

In spite of the promise of what in India is called a "Europe morning"—*i.e.*, getting up late — I awoke at daylight and soon turned out. The mist was as thick as ever, and after a little, the wind getting up, the dust began to fly, which scattered our hopes of a quiet day in camp. At about ten o'clock Baratbai announced distinguished visitors. They turned out to be the headmen of Kugiar. We spread a big *munda* in front of my tent, as it was the largest in the camp, and then went out to meet them, led them up in due form, and begged them to be seated. They brought us a welcome present of melons, for which we were very grateful, not having tasted fruit or vegetables for a long time. We then ordered tea, which was passed round, and having concluded ceremonies, they proceeded to business.

The Beg said that he had come, as was his duty, to offer us all he had, and at the same time to ask us who we were, where we came from, where we were going, what our caravan consisted of, how many horses we had, how many servants, and last, but not least, to see our passports. We thanked him much for his civility, and told him we were not traders, but simple sportsmen, proceeding to Sirikul by the shortest route, there to shoot the *Ovis poli* called in Turki *goolja;* that having done so, we intended to go to Yarkand, and spend the winter in the plains of Turkistan; that I was furnished with a passport from Pekin to pass me all over the dominion, and that this passport enabled me to take a friend with me, pointing to Bower. I then produced the precious document, which, being written in Chinese, was quite unintelligible to them; but the sight of it proved satisfactory, and they took leave, going off to have a talk with our followers, to find out, probably, if we had been speaking the truth—for, of course, they could not understand why we undertook such an arduous journey just to kill a beast or two.

On September the 1st we were up at daylight, and just starting, when the head of the *karaol* appeared, and begged us not to go through the town of Kugiar, as he had strict orders from the Amban of Yarkand that no travellers were to pass that way. This was rather disappointing, as we wished to see the place; besides which, we heard that the alternative road led over a pretty high ridge. They told us that over the ridge was much the quickest way; for if we went by Kugiar, we had to go down to the end of this ridge, and then turn up the Tiznaf valley at right angles, and the road therefore was twice as long.

We ascended the ridge by a winding ravine, and kept thinking that every sky-line we saw meant the summit, only to be disappointed time after time. At last we got on to a sort of tableland, and there the path branched off in various directions. The country seemed easy enough as long as we kept on the plateau, but when we got into a ravine and began to descend, the aspect began to look grave. We got involved in a narrow precipitous nullah, which every now and again became so confined at the bottom, and so steep at the sides, that we had to drive our ponies up side nullahs and go round to avoid bad places. Time went on, the poor ponies began to show signs of having had enough of it, and the prospect of being benighted where we were was anything but cheering, as there was no water, no fuel to cook food, and no grass for the ponies.

Bower and I (Dauvergne had left us) decided that there must be a path somewhere, and the only thing to do was to find it; so, halting the caravan, we set out to explore. At first it looked hopeless: we found ourselves in a complete network of ravines and ridges as far as we could see. The Tiznaf valley was not far off, and the Kugiaris had declared there was a path somewhere, if we could only find it; so we determined to ascend a spur and stick to it until we came across a track. By good luck, after climbing a bit, we found the welcome path, and having dragged the ponies up with some difficulty, we went on, determined not to leave until we reached the place to which it led. It was getting dusk by the time we left the hill, and got on to what appeared to be a flat, stony, barren valley, where we could hear a river, but could not see it. When we left the last ridge the path turned sharp to the east, our course over the ridge having been generally north, and so far as we could see there were no signs of cultivation or habitation. We could make out two or three beasts, evidently laden with *burtsa* (fuel), ahead of us on the path, so we concluded that a village was not far off. On catching them up, the driver told us that if we kept the road we should be at Tiznaf very shortly. At last we got to the edge of a pretty high cliff, and there, like the Israelites of old, we saw the promised land at our feet. The river had cut its way in this valley, forming a fertile bottom about half a mile wide, leaving a sort of shelf on each side, on one of which we had been travelling.

I never was so glad to get to the end of a march, as our ponies were dead beat, and it was nearly dark. We pitched our tents in what appeared to be a fallow-field close to the village. Some of the natives turned up at once, and brought fuel, and *boosa* (chaff) for the ponies, which was all we required; of water there was abundance. We got our dinner at about ten o'clock, and decided that we must halt the next day and rest our ponies.

Daylight awoke me, and I got up at once to see what sort of place we were in. We were camped just on the edge of cultivation. Up and down the valley as far as eye could reach were green fields of Indian corn, millet, peas, mustard, &c., interspersed with groves of walnut, poplar, and aspen trees, with here and there an orchard of apricot and apple trees, to say nothing of melon-plants and vines all about the cottages. It did, indeed, appear a land of plenty. After walking about for a while and feasting my eyes on the scene, I began to think it time for breakfast, so returned to camp and found the dreams that my imagination had conjured up realised. Quite a crowd of natives had come with melons, apricots, grapes, apples, eggs, and milk—in fact, all that the heart of a traveller could desire; so opening my pack of cotton-stuff, I distributed coloured handkerchiefs, bits of cotton prints, and so on, right and left to the villagers, who were just as delighted with them as we were with the fruit. This was the village of Ushlaich, situated at an altitude of 6000 feet.

In the evening I put my trout-rod together and started off to see what the Tiznaf river would produce. Not a fish would move in the main river,—I fancy the water was too cold,—but in a side-stream, artificially made for irrigating purposes, where the water was warmer, I caught as many as I wanted; nothing bigger than six inches in length, but good enough to eat, and better than nothing to catch. I was of course watched by a crowd, who were astonished at my rod, gut, and flies. The fish was a *barbus* of some sort, very like the Kashmir so-called trout.

Proceeding down this lovely valley for a mile or two, and then turning west, after a short ascent we found ourselves once more in a desert. A long wearisome march it proved, over a barren plateau, not a blade of grass or a drop of water all the way. The mist, which had hung over all for the last few days, now cleared off, and we were able to see what was before us. We seemed to be crossing the base of spurs that ran down from the high mountain region to our south or west. To the north and east appeared the desert plains of this part of Turkistan, and a very desolate country it looked. It was quite late in the evening when, on emerging from a close gorge which we had followed for the last two miles, we came suddenly into a valley exactly similar to the Tisnaf, and camped at a village called Uyoung, which we made out to be about the same altitude as the last. We had no sooner got there than the headman came and said that during our stay we must be his guests, that he would supply us with all we wanted, and prayed of us to halt the next day. This we decided to do, for the march of twenty-six miles had been very hard on the ponies, owing to heat and want of water.

We had many visitors and presents of fruit, &c., during the day. Our host was most kind, and asked permission to entertain our servants at a *dusterkhan*, consisting of tea-bread and sweetmeats, in his house; for which we thanked him, and said we also should pay him a visit, which pleased him much. In the evening he came to our camp to ask us not to start very early the next morning, as he had received a message to say that a Beg would arrive with a Chinese interpreter from Kargalik to see our passport and give us every assistance in his power—in other words, to find out all about us.

The Usbashi, or headman of the village, came when we were striking our tents, and said that the Beg had come during the night and would visit us shortly; so we spread a carpet for his accommodation and got out the passport. He was accompanied by a miserable-looking Chinaman, whose duty it was to read and take note of the passport. The language of the country is old Turkish, but educated people speak Persian. The Beg turned out to be a capital fellow, and seemed to know all about English manners and customs. . He had been in the Kilian fort for a long time, and had met Dalgleish once or twice: he it was who took the fakir who was with Dad Mahomed when he committed the murder. After some general conversation, he asked us kindly to give him information relative to the composition of our caravan and future movements, so that he might inform the Amban of Kargalik. Having drawn up his report, he asked permission to depart, which we graciously accorded, being in a hurry to be off ourselves. We then presented the Usbashi who had been so civil with a *lungi* or turban, and a few odds and ends of cotton goods, and once more were *en route*.

We followed the valley for about fourteen miles, throughout which cultivation and little hamlets appeared at intervals all the way, and camped in a grove of willows, whose shade we found very grateful, as the sun, since we had got rid of the mist, was powerfully hot. About nine miles farther we turned up a tributary valley from the west, which we followed for five miles; then hearing from our guide that we left it to ascend a pretty high range, decided to camp, there being water and other necessaries, and commence the ascent the next day.

Ascending a steepish narrow ravine for about six miles, we came to a small village of *yurts*. Here we found an intelligent man, Sultan Beg by name, who had come from Wakhan by the road we intended to follow. He offered to go back and show us the road; and as he spoke Hindostani, we were delighted to have him. There being no room for our camp near his *yurt* at the bottom of the ravine, he led us up the side of the mountain to a flat bit of prairie, covered with grass, where there was a lovely view of green hills all round, with woods of pine, juniper, and mountain-ash. It was a wonderful contrast to what we had been accustomed to, and reminded us strongly of Kashmir. Bower and I went up towards this pass in the evening, and enjoyed our walk immensely: the smell of the pines and juniper in the woods was a better tonic than any produced by a doctor.

Early next morning we found Barat trying to do a deal with some Wakhis for a couple of new ponies, and after some haggling he got hold of a nice one, which I determined to annex for my own riding. How he got round the man I cannot imagine, for he gave him a terrible cripple and five rupees in exchange! To our disappointment Sultan Beg did not turn up. However, another man who had come to the camp said he would guide us as far as Langar. Our way was by the path we had explored in the evening, to the top of the pass Tahta Dawan, 15,000 feet, pine-woods and grass-prairies all the way—a nice easy ascent. The descent was more abrupt. At first the path led through pine-woods; but after a little we left these behind, and got on to the same bare rocky mountains that we were accustomed to see, for about seven miles, until the ravine merged into a larger valley that came from the west. Following this for three miles, we arrived at a fort and *karaol* called Egizarak Kurgaon.[1]

As we followed the river, which ran into nice little nooks, I had spotted some fair-sized fish; so as soon as we had pitched camp, I up with my rod and started off, and had a capital evening's sport with an alder-fly, fishing it dry and catching a lot, for they rose beautifully.

Dauvergne had joined us on the line of march again, and with him we found our faithless friend Sultan Beg, near whose *yurt* he had pitched his camp. He was off ahead of us in the morning. We had a gradual ascent to the Arpalik Dawan, about 10,000 feet, from the top of which, looking north and west, appeared a massive range of mountainous rock falling sheer down on every side, too steep to support any soil or vegetation. On descending we found a gigantic gorge with a wall of rock rising on each side of us, and so precipitous that the sun was only visible for a very short time in the valley. These gorges, our guide

[1] *Kurgaon* means fort.

told us, were the features of the mountain-chain through which the Zarafshan (Yarkand) river flowed. We inquired if there was a road along this river. He replied, "Oh no, there are no banks; the river at every turn washes up against the sides of the gorge through which it flows."

At about five o'clock we got to our destination, a small village called Langar. Here we found Dauvergne camped in an orchard of apricot and walnut trees. He had been in some time, and had sent over word to the Hakim Beg[1] at Tung to make arrangements for a *zakh*, or raft, supported on inflated goatskins, to take his kit across on the morrow. So we told Barat to get out the skins which we had brought for such an emergency, and make arrangements for transit the next day.

Having fortified ourselves with a cup of tea, and settled our camp, Bower and I walked down to the river, which we could hear roaring below. It was at that time a mighty torrent, and looked most uncompromising; but it had to be crossed somehow. They told us that about a mile above our camp there was a long flat reach where we

---

[1] The governor of the province of Sirikul, into which you enter after crossing the Zarafshan.

could float our raft across. In the late autumn and winter it ran low, and was fordable in many places. The gorge through which it runs is, I think, the finest I ever saw, and even beats that of the Chimdra Baga, in Pangi,—huge mountains of black rock rising sheer up on each side, and so narrow that the river seems to have cut its way through.

Meanwhile Barat had made arrangements with some men whose business it was to ferry across the river, unpacked the skins, and cut some poles to form the raft, so that there was nothing further to be done until morning. We got up early, and found that Barat had gone to the ferry to put the raft together. He left word for us not to hurry, as it would take some time; so we breakfasted at our ease before striking camp, then loading up the ponies, we went to the crossing-place. There we found quite a crowd assembled on the opposite side, of all the principal men of Sirikul, who lived at a place called Tung, situated on a small river of that name in the valley in which the town stood. The Hakim Beg, or governor of the province, was conspicuous amongst them; also the Shan Beggi, or vice-governor, and various other big men of sorts, all attired in their best *chogas*, with gold-laced *lungis* or turbans on their heads. They had come down to receive us in due form. Barat said he knew them all, and told us that when we interviewed the Hakim Beg we must be careful not to excite him in any way, for he was rather mad, and inclined to be violent at times. He had on several occasions killed people on the spur of the moment in a fit of passion; and on no account should we give him a loaded revolver, as he might try its effects on some unfortunate individual!

We found our raft ready, and the Mullahs who were to conduct it across in attendance, so set to work to load it for the first trip. It seemed rather a frail craft for the work, formed of a dozen inflated goatskins, lashed together by a slight frame of green willow-poles on the top. On this frame were placed four *molis*, or pack-saddles, which are stuffed with dry grass, and made a very good floor to the raft, and on it we put our first consignment of cargo, about 220 lb. weight. These we lashed down securely with ropes, and a man was told off to sprawl over the top and keep all as snug as possible. When we launched our raft, we soon found the use of the floor of *molis*, as the raft swam pretty deep when fully laden, and without them our goods and chattels would have got soaked through. Having proceeded so far, I asked how the raft was to be got across, for I saw no paddles or oars of any kind, such as are used in Kashmir and other parts. Barat replied, "Oh, that is the ponies' business; you will soon see how it is done." Bower's riding-pony, which happened to be the most suitable, was caught, and after some trouble forced into the river in front of the raft as it lay alongside of the shore, which was here rather abrupt. He was taken by the head by one of the Mullahs, who was mounted on an inflated goatskin; his tail was then made fast to a tow-rope fixed to the raft, and he was headed by his driver, who swam alongside across the stream! Rather a novel sort of propeller, but it worked admirably. The stream took them down about 100 yards, when the pony found his legs and hauled the raft up on the opposite shore. Having discharged its cargo, the raft returned in the same way to our bank, and landed 200 yards below. This was the slowest part of the proceeding, for it had to be worked back up-stream to the point of departure. It was then loaded and ferried across as before.

On its second trip I got on to the raft, thinking that it would be well to go and discourse with the swells on the opposite shore. Being rather a wet performance, I took off my shoes and stockings, rolled up my trousers, and committed myself to the deep. The raft swam rather low in the water, and as we neared the opposite shore it stranded, so I jumped off to relieve the weight, and waded ashore. I was received with much ceremony as I stepped out of the river, and was bidden to sit down on a *munda* which had been spread for my accommodation.

I tried to look dignified as I waded ashore, but fear I did not succeed, for the stones were very rough and hard to the naked feet, and trousers rolled up to the knee did not add to the effect. However, I squatted down and looked dignified to the best of my ability.

Of course, after the first civil speeches had been got over, the usual "Who are you?" "Where are you going?" "What have you come for?" and all the rest of it, began. I replied that I had received permission and a passport from the Emperor at Pekin to travel all about the country, shoot, and collect specimens of animals; that for this purpose I was going first of all to Taghdumbash Pamir, and that I had travelled by this road in order that I might see the Hakim Beg of Sirikul, of whose greatness and kindness I had heard so much, and so on. I had very nearly got through my *répertoire* of humbug when fortunately Bower landed, and a rush was made for him, and he took up the running, whilst I was left in peace. When he was played out Dauvergne came, and so we kept our friends occupied, showing them odds and ends, watches, pipes, pocket-knives, &c., until, having satisfied their curiosity, we thought we might as well get rid of them, so suggested that the day was getting on and they had a long way to go home,—that we would follow them to Tung as soon as we had got our things across the river; and so, to our great relief, they went, with the promise that we should visit them in due form next day. Dauvergne crossed all his things with only one turn over, which, bar getting the cargo wet and tipping one of his servants into the river, did no harm. Ours was a longer job, as our combined kit was greater than his, and it was dusk before the last load was landed and the ponies across. However, we got under way as quickly as possible, had a stiff climb over a cliff, and then a mile of flat, which brought us to the Tung river, which we forded, and as it was by then quite dark, pitched our camp on a convenient place, and turned in, very much relieved at having got across the great Zarafshan without a mishap.

Everything was in a mess and wet, so we took it easily in the morning and started about eleven, following the Tung river along a nice easy path for eight miles, chiefly through cultivated fields and orchards, to Tung, where we found Dauvergne encamped. Having put on our best clothes, such as they were, we started off in a body, servants and all, to call on the Hakim Beg. It has often struck me that we travellers in the East make a great mistake in not taking something better in the way of clothes for swell occasions. We seem to have a special objection to anything of the sort. Each trip I vow I will do so, but at the last moment the garments are put aside, and I go off with nothing better than a shooting-suit. I had taken the trouble to bring some uniform from England, fully intending to astonish the natives of Turkistan with my magnificence, but at the last moment left it, with that stupid English feeling, "Why should

I dress myself up for a Chinaman or any other savage?"

When we approached the viceregal lodge of the Hakim Beg, he came out to meet us, and showed us into his durbar—a large room with a platform all round, spread with carpets, where we were invited to squat. The proper way to do so in this country is to kneel down and sit on your heels. We found this not only difficult but very painful, so apologised to our host, telling him that no doubt we had been badly brought up, and so could not do what was right and proper. He was very polite, saying that he did not wonder at it, for he had heard that the *Faringi* (European) always sat in a chair, and he regretted much he had none to offer us.

We were then served with a *dusterkhan*, consisting of a boiled sheep cut into quarters. As etiquette demands that the whole of the animal should be placed before you, it presents rather an appalling dish, especially when you have just breakfasted; besides which, no plates or forks are used,—you have to cut off the limb of the animal and gnaw it like a dog! We had a good excuse for our abstinence ready, as the Hakim Beg had sent us a present of fruit and bread shortly before; so we told him that we found these things so good, and had eaten so freely of them, that we could not possibly eat any more, but that we would take it away with us and eat it later in the day. Our servants, meanwhile, seated on the other side of the room, had been presented with another sheep, of which they made short work, and thoroughly enjoyed themselves. When we had sat for half an hour and partaken of tea, we presented the Hakim Beg with a *choga* of silk, and to each of his assistants a gold *lungi;* then thanking him for his hospitality, asked leave to depart.

As soon as I got back to camp I put my trout-rod together and had a try at the river. The fish were rather shy, but I got half a dozen, the largest rather over 1 lb. in weight. They were of two sorts, one similar to the Kashmir fish, the other very like the mahaseer in shape, but with small scales, and of a general bluish colour, with small teeth in the gills and larger ones in the throat, exactly like the mahaseer.

We had now no need of a guide, as Barat said he knew the country from this to the Pamirs perfectly. I found Dauvergne had engaged yaks to carry his things over the pass, and told Barat to do likewise, but he put it off till the next camp. We had only got a mile out when we were stopped at the house of the Shan Beggi, who insisted on our partaking of a *dusterkhan* similar to yesterday's, sheep and all.

From being fairly good at first, the road as we went along the valley grew narrower, and we had to ford the river at every bend, which was hard on the ponies, and I regretted we had not the yaks to relieve them. At the camping-ground Barat said he would now make arrangements for some, and as in the course of the afternoon a few did turn up, I thought the bargain was concluded. No yaks were to be seen in the morning, and on asking where they where, Barat explained the terms were too exorbitant, and he would get them during the day, or at the next camp. I was very angry, and gave him a bit of my mind, but there was nothing to be done but load the ponies and make the best of them.

It was terribly bad going, having to cross the river times innumerable, the fords getting worse and worse, the bottom being composed of large boulders, over which the ponies had to struggle, and frequently came down. The valley got wilder as we proceeded, and the hill-tops opened out, having snow on their summits, but with beautiful grassy slopes lower down. It looked like excellent ibex-ground, but no one had ever shot over it. Here and there we saw big flocks of sheep and goats on the downs, and in the bottom an occasional *yurt* of the shepherds. Dauvergne, who was already encamped, gave us a cup of tea, for which we were very grateful after the worry of the road. The ponies came in late dead beat, entailing a halt on the next day.

Dauvergne started early to cross the Kolkandhar Pass, and we were left in the lurch. However, there was a man who was said to have some yaks, and we sent for him. He tried to make excuses, but when asked point-blank his reasons for refusing, said that Sultan Beg, Dauvergne's guide, had told him that if he took service with me I should beat him on the road! Naturally I was rather put out, and had I been able to lay hands on Mr Sultan Beg, he would have remembered it. His reason, no doubt, was enmity with Barat, there having been a feud for a long time between the servants of our two caravans— no unusual occurrence when two parties travel long together. I told him he was a fool to believe what he was told by a liar like Sultan

Beg; that I would pay him at once for the yaks, and answer for it that no one should touch him on the road. On these terms he promised to supply us with what beasts he had, and in the evening four yaks turned up.

Just behind our camp the path led over a very steep slope, up which the ponies scrambled, but hustled each other a little as they got near the top: one lost his footing, and fell back head over heels, a fearful cropper, down to the bottom in about three bounds. We ran down expecting to find every bone in his body broken, but when we got his load off he staggered to his feet, very much cut about, but otherwise unhurt: the tent with which he was laden had saved him. After a while he gave himself a shake, which meant he was all right; so we put on his load again, and he soon caught up the others!

About mid-day we got into a hollow where there was a small lake, and beyond saw our path winding up to the summit of the pass, apparently at no great distance; but we soon realised it was both farther and steeper than it looked, for it led up a slope of shale which gave no foothold to the animals, and one after another they subsided as if the life had gone out of them. The altitude prevented their getting their wind, and we had regularly to haul them up without any loads, the yaks doing the whole of the work in several trips. Altogether it took four hours to get everything to the top over this bit, which could not have measured 300 yards. Bower tried to take the altitude with his boiling-point thermometer, but the wind prevented the water boiling, and he had to give it up. The height could have been little less than 18,000 feet. The view was very fine, and the most extended we had had for long. Far away in the north we made out what we afterwards found to be Pargarma Peak: at our feet lay a broad valley, down which and northwards was our road; while to the west appeared a sort of pamir, broken up by low hills, which looked very like Ovis-ground.

We were now within three marches of Taghdumbash,—one to the valley below us, one over the range facing, called the Karatagh or black mountains, and the last up the river Tashkurgan to Taghdumbash. This was a cheering prospect, and so the ponies seemed to think. The slopes on this side became more and more gradual, and they jogged down the path merrily. At five o'clock they thought they had earned their tea, for coming to a patch of green turf, a sign of water, they made for it. The yak-drivers, however, recommended a camp farther on; so they had to be content with the promise of better things to come, and we soon reached the spot, where there was grass, water, and fuel.

During the night snow fell to the depth of three inches, but the warm sun quickly melted it; so, dismissing our yak-drivers with a small present of cotton-stuff, we started down the valley, which soon showed signs of cultivation. Here and there were little hamlets of mud-huts, and fields of wheat and barley, as yet quite green.

On that day's march we saw the first signs of the animals of which we were in search—*Ovis poli* horns amongst a heap of others, ibex and burrel: they were beside a *mazar* or shrine by the roadside,—not very large ones, but it showed we were approaching their habitat. The villagers told us that in the winter they were to be seen now and again on the hills between us and Taghdumbash.

I tried the river that evening, but without success. Bower, who had taken his gun to a small bog near, had better luck, getting a couple of snipe and several blue pigeons. We had a try next morning at another bog; I had only a shot at a snipe, but Bower got a couple and some teal. When we got back to camp, a man brought up a very nice pony, which I promptly bought, after some haggling, for 150 rupees, a top price in this country; but I took a great fancy to the animal, a well-shaped dark bay, 13.3, without a white spot, so did not grudge the money.

We were just going to sit down to dinner when we saw a crowd of people approaching full tilt. It proved to be the Beg of Tashkurgan and his followers, so we had to postpone our repast and go through the usual ceremonies, giving him tea and showing the passport. He was quite a boy, barely twenty, a son of the Hakim Beg of Sirikul. After a little talk we told him we would not detain him, and sent him off with a present of a gold-laced *lungi*.

We were anxious to be off early next morning, but found the yaks Barat had arranged for had not appeared. He was at his old game of cutting down prices, for when I produced the rupees demanded they turned up immediately.

After descending the valley a short distance, we found ourselves on a small table-land which took us to the base of the range of hills dividing us from the Tashkurgan valley. The ascent of these was easy but tedious; we had hoped at the col for a sight of the Pamir; but the path took us down a winding ravine, the ridge of which, rising to a good height on both sides, blocked the view. At about 3 P.M. we reached the mouth of the ravine and entered the valley of the Tashkurgan river, commonly called the Sarikol Pamir.

This valley, about twelve to fourteen miles across, descends gradually from the ranges on either side in stony moraines to the river, which flows in the centre. About six miles below we saw our camping-ground, which in the distance looked like a patch of jungle; and farther again we could distinguish the fort of Tashkurgan,— literally translated, Fort of Stone.

On the other side of the range, on the opposite side of the river, lay the Little Pamir; and the upper part of the valley, which we were now to ascend, was called Taghdumbash Pamir.

The camp was on a cliff overlooking the river, at the sight of which, as a fisherman, my heart warmed. What a salmon-river it would have made, running into lovely pools at every turn! In colour it was like blue crystal; but not a sign of a fish could I see, although in 20 feet of water

I could count every stone at the bottom. As night was coming on, we set to work to collect *burtsa*, and soon had a goodly pile ready for Mr Rahimadar, the Kashmiri cook, so that soon after the caravan came in our dinner was ready.

These Kashmiri servants (and this one in particular) are excellent people for this sort of work. They go anywhere with you, ask no questions, and follow like dogs. They will walk the whole day, and as soon as they arrive in camp, wet or dry, sun or snow, they set to work to light your fire and make you a dinner, however scarce may be the fuel or the victuals. To-day I reckoned our march at twenty miles.

The next morning we found our tents frozen stiff as a board from having been packed wet the previous day, so we had to wait for the sun to get up and thaw them before resuming our march. All down the valley we had showers of sleet and snow, and after going about fifteen miles, we camped near a group of Kirghiz *yurts*, the people very civilly bringing us milk, *dahi* (butter-milk), and clotted cream—a great addition to our usual fare.

Crossing a tributary stream, we followed the main river to an old fort called Kurgaon-i-Ujadba, then forded the Tashkurgan river, and went due west until we entered a valley which led down from the Karachunkar Pass.

We were now in what may be called the extreme westerly corner of Chinese territory, the range on the west dividing us from Wakhan. About three miles up this valley we came to the tent of the Beg of the district, a Kirghiz, Kutch Mahomed, who is stationed here as a sort of agent between the Kunjuts and the Chinese; and it was to him we were to apply for shikaris and guides to show us sport in the neighbourhood.

Dauvergne had already arrived, and told us that, after shooting a few days up the valley, he should cross the Karachunkar Pass into Wakhan on his way back to Kashmir *via* Chitral.

Kutch Mahomed soon came to pay us a visit, and kindly promised to do all he could for us. He was very anxious we should remain a few days at his *yurt*, placing all he had at our disposal. We assured him we were most grateful for his kind offer, but were keen to get at the poli, and should prefer if he would allow us to pay him a visit on our return. All we asked in the meantime were shikaris to show us the ground. He brought us over a couple of sheep, butter-milk, and cream. Giving him our thanks, we presented him with a *choga*, placing it on his back with our own hands, which pleased him much, as it is in this way you show honour to a guest in the East.

It was snowing hard at daylight, so we waited until nine o'clock, when it cleared off. We had not gone many miles when we came upon another Kirghiz camp, and were again entertained. As we travelled on, the valley gradually opened out, the slopes on each side becoming less precipitous, and more like what we took to be poli-ground. There were, we were told, plenty of arkar, or female *Ovis poli*, in the hills, but for the goolja, or male, we must go higher up the valley. Coming to a grassy patch, we determined to camp, as the Beg had told us it would be impossible to reach the hunting-ground in one march. After going some six miles or so next morning, we came on the track of poli, but only small arkars. The shikaris said we must go higher up the ravines and mountain-sides for the gooljas. Finding a good place, we settled the camp, and I started up the hill, burning to get sight of my first poli. My hopes were soon realised; for after a couple of miles up the slopes, I saw some dots in the far distance, and turned the glass on them. Poli at last! Giving the glass to the shikari, I asked him what they were. He could make nothing of them; but when we got nearer, I made them out clearly to be females. Excepting in colour—for they were darker brown on the back and whiter on the legs and belly—they were just like the female *Ovis Ammon*. I saw no males near them; so after watching them graze awhile, I went back, and we turned in, big with hopes for the morrow.

We were off before daylight, Bower following the main range, while I took the same direction as on the previous evening. The herd were in the same place; and after getting close enough to have a good look, left them undisturbed, and went on up the nullah. I did not like the ground at all; it was too precipitous, and not my idea of poli-ground—that is to say, comparing it with the habitat of the *Ovis Ammon*, the male of which species generally frequents open undulating hills, the females only being found on the more precipitous mountain-sides. I kept on for some distance, looking carefully for fresh tracks; and seeing none, I concluded that at this season, at all events, the great sheep sought his food elsewhere, so retracing my steps, I got back to camp about three o'clock. There I found Bower's shikari without his master. He told me that Bower had got a shot at a herd of gooljas, and thinking he had wounded one, had gone after it as hard as he could—so fast indeed that he (the shikari) could not follow. I told him I thought he had behaved very badly, as Bower might lose his way and get benighted on the mountain. He said he was sorry, but not being a good walker, he could not possibly keep up with the sahib. I soon found out this was a fact: the Kirghiz, as a rule, cannot walk a bit, and generally when hunting ride a pony or yak. I was on the point of sending him off when Bower appeared. He had been led a terrible dance, right on to the top of the range which bounded the valley. The beasts were moving, and he was not steady, but thought he had wounded one: they did not stop, but travelled on, so that he could just keep them within sight. On crossing a spur he ran into full view of another herd, and immediately unslinging his rifle, banged off right and left, but without effect. Meanwhile he had lost sight of the first herd, and as the stony ground showed no tracks, gave them up in despair. Fortunately he had taken his bearings as he went, and so got in all right. So much for our first attempts!

We were off again next morning, separating as before and taking the same line of country. There were the female herd in much the same spot, but below I could see a few more. Before putting the glasses on them, I thought they were gooljas, for they looked even at that distance quite different in shape and colour. As soon as I sighted them in the glass there was no doubt about it. Gooljas they were, seven of them. They were lying in a sort of basin, and, as far as I could make out, quite unapproachable; and there was nothing for it but to wait patiently till they moved. The hollow plain on which they lay, after ascending a bit, fell abruptly in the valley. If they would but get up and graze their way within shot of this edge, I had them; but if they moved in the other, there was nothing but open easy slopes, which would not afford the slightest cover for a stalk. As they did not seem in any hurry to move, I thought that in case they did as I wished them to do, I would take time by the forelock and meet them halfway; so I worked round the edge of the plateau, taking a look over now and again to see what they were up to. At last one got up, and, stretching himself, began to graze. One after another followed suit, and, to my great joy, moved quietly in my direction. I really began to think that the dream of my life was about to be realised, and I was to kill my first poli. I made up my mind to be very steady, and, when the time came, pick out the best of the lot. While watching them intently with this object, all of a sudden up went their heads, they wheeled round, paused for a second, gazing intently, then away they stretched at full gallop right across the plain, and did not pause till well up the mountain-side.

What was it?

Why, a beast of a wolf, half a mile off, trotting along with his tongue hanging out! Oh, why, oh, why were such vermin ever invented? If only *he* had been within shot! The herd of females had also seen him, and huddled themselves up together. There must have been a hundred of them, packed as close as a herd of tame sheep. I passed within 300 yards of them, in full view, but they only wheeled about, and did not seem to dread me at all. This, for some occult reason, I have always found to be the case. If you do not intend to shoot at certain animals, they always seem to know it, be they *Ovis Ammon*, ibex, markhor, burrel, or what not. I have sat down within 200 or 300 yards of a herd, and after staring at me or circling round, they have begun to graze, or even lain down in front of me.

After lunch I wandered about, but saw no fresh tracks. Every now and again a most intensely cold blast came down the valley, accompanied by fine snow which almost blinded me,— so, thinking the sport not good enough, I turned back.

Bower soon after came in. He had watched a herd of gooljas all day in a most unapproachable place, and they had at last moved off where he could not follow. We held a consultation as to a change of ground with the shikaris, who recommended a move up the main valley where two branch nullahs came down.

Dauvergne, we found, was camped in another called Kukturuk, which, they said, was the best place for good heads. Where we were, as a rule, heads were good; but the ground had been much disturbed by the Kirghiz from the Little Pamirs, who constantly came over to hunt—there having been much sickness amongst the Ovis in their own part, and scarcely any left. This epidemic, they told us, occurs about once in twenty years, and the reason it does not spread into the Taghdumbash is, that the grass is so much better and more plentiful than on the other Pamirs.

The shikaris asked permission to shoot females on the way. We did not much like the idea; but as we were more or less dependent on them, we thought it well to keep them in good-humour, and they started off in the middle of the night.

As we got higher up the valley, there were a lot of poli-heads lying about, mostly very fine specimens, very few small ones, and hardly any females. These, Barat explained, had been killed by wolves. Being weak in the winter from scarcity of food, those with heavy heads were easily run down, whereas the small rams and females were able to hold their own.

As we travelled over the foot-hills, we kicked up a hare at almost every step, blue in colour, like the Scotch mountain-hare. Our dogs—Joker my black spaniel, and Waffles, a nondescript fox-terrier of Bower's—were always on the run. Needless to say, they never caught one, but it was impossible to keep them to heel. As soon as we got them in, another hare would start up, and they were off again.

After going about six miles we found ourselves on a good grass flat, at the top of the main valley, up which we had been working. This was a favourable place to stop at, as Barat said there were some fine beats in various directions, while there was grass and fuel for camp necessaries.

The shikaris did not cast up until mid-day, without, however, having had a shot; and when, at 4 P.M., we sent for them, intending to have a try up the mountain, they said they were much too tired to go, and wanted to cook some food. We began to think our Kirghiz gillies a bad bargain, but concluded we had better not run them too hard at first, or they might leave us in the lurch. Bower said he would go alone; and Jaffer, my servant, saying he would like to have a sight of a goolja, I gave him my rifle, and we started off. At the mouth of the nullah, Bower took the left spur and I the right. It looked a very likely place, having good patches of green grass, and a small stream running along the bottom. When we had scrambled up the stony ridge, and began to get blown, Jaffer was glad to sit down, as he found his breath short at these high altitudes, so I got out the glasses, and very soon made out Bower on the other side, about the same height. Presently I heard some stones rattle down the opposite slope, and saw seven gooljas, who appeared to be descending to the bottom, probably for their evening meal; and after looking about to see if the coast was clear, they began to graze. They then worked up the valley, and I determined to go in a similar direction, so that if they caught sight of Bower, who was moving along on the sky-line, and who had evidently not seen them, I should be handy, and get a shot as they crossed my way. This was my only chance, for the wind was blowing right up the nullah.

It was hard work scrambling over the abrupt stony slopes of broken quartz, keeping our bodies as low as possible amongst the stones, and lying quite still in all sorts of uncomfortable positions when any of the poli raised their heads to look about. After a while they seemed to get uneasy, then all of a sudden made up their minds and turned up the slope on which we were. My hopes were done for, as they would now pass at least 400 yards in front of where I lay, and there was no cover; besides, as soon as they got to my level they would get my wind. My chance of a shot being over, I made up my mind to study the effect and spread of scent at a certain distance. I reckoned that if they came on straight, they would pass exactly 400 yards in front, with the wind directly in my rear. They came on slowly, exactly in the line I expected, and when within about 100 yards of the point I had marked as being straight down wind, the leading ram threw up his head, sniffed the wind in my direction, and set off up the mountain-side at a gallop, the rest following. They were all good heads; but, I consoled myself, no shot was better than a miss. I verified the distance, and found that 80 yards below the direct line of wind the Ovis had got my scent, 400 yards from where I was, which gave the spread at that distance 160 yards. The strength of the wind was normal, the usual draught, which blows *down* the valleys in the morning and *up* as soon as the sun rises.

CHAPTER V.

AMONG THE PAMIRS.

WE VISIT DAUVERGNE'S CAMP—A SUCCESSFUL STALK—DEAD BEAT—DAUVERGNE LEAVES—THE KILIK VALLEY—A TANTALISING SHOT—MESSAGE FROM GROMCHEFSKI—AN AVALANCHE—AKAL JAHN PROVIDES SHIKARIS—MORE OVES—BOWER'S SUCCESS—AN ICE WALL—COLLECTING THE SPOILS —TEA WITH GROMCHEFSKI.

THE next morning it was snowing hard, and bed was the best place; but as it showed signs of clearing by eight o'clock, I shouted to Bower if he was ready for breakfast, and turned out. As we were discussing our programme over our pipes, two Kirghiz mounted on ponies came in, bringing a note from Dauvergne and some *Ovis poli* meat. He had, he said, great luck the previous day, killing three good gooljas; that there were plenty more in the nullah, and as he was leaving for Wakhan in a couple of days, we had better come up and camp with him at once.

Now, moving camp in a snowstorm is not a pleasant diversion; so we determined to walk over and see him, leaving our tents until next day. We found him very busy with his heads and skins, with which he was well satisfied. He intended to start for Chitral in a couple of days, fearing, if he delayed, the passes would be closed by snow. After spending an hour or two with him, we returned to our camp. The snow had ceased, but the mist hung thick on the hill.

We laid our plans overnight. The day broke clear, the air crisp, and, with snow on the ground, it was a grand morning to spot game. I very soon ascended the slope of the steppe, which occurs all round the base of the mountains, and had hardly got one eye over the top when I spotted a herd of poli. They showed up well on the snow, and with the aid of my glass I counted twenty, all rams. It looked as if I was to get my chance at last, as they were all busy digging through the snow, which lay about 4 inches deep, to get at the grass beneath.

The edge of the steppe was undulating, and I soon made out a line that should take me within shot; so, telling my Kirghiz to lie quite still— really the only thing these people are good at—

set to work to crawl along the snow, casting an eye over the spur to see that the herd were all right. It was slow work, and very cold for the hands, and I had taken off my sheepskin gloves to be ready for a shot. The cover was not high enough for me to move on my feet, even crouching, so I had to go on all-fours, as it were, on my elbows and toes. Having reached the last hillock that afforded cover, I determined to take my chance. It was a longer shot than I reckoned, rather more than 200 yards; but as I could see no better stalk, and as it was getting very cold, I tried to make up my mind which to fire at. They were all pretty close together; but, as I was hesitating, one walked out a little apart from the rest and turned his head. Seeing it was a pretty good one, I gave him the preference, and, after a careful aim, fired. The smoke hung for a moment, so that I saw nothing; but when it cleared, they were all on their legs. They had taken a short spurt, and paused, as they often do, for a moment after a shot, so I gave them the other barrel. This time there was no mistake; I heard the bullet tell, and as they made off, one remained behind. He did not fall at once, but moved on slowly. Presently he lay down, and I went round, and approached from behind, thinking he might want another shot; but he was quite dead. In working up to him, I crossed the line of No. 1, and saw by the blood-tracks that he also was hit, but had disappeared with the rest of the herd. I tracked him for some way, but concluding I should have to follow a considerable distance, I went back to have a look at the other, and was disappointed to find his head only measured 44 inches.

Sending the Kirghiz off to camp for a pony to take it back, I slung my rifle and went off up the mountain, determined to stick to the wounded one until he was brought to hand. The blood-tracks were well defined, but always with the herd. At last I came within sight of them, and with my glass made out the hindermost one was dead lame. I followed on, though very done, the ascent being steep and stony, and the rifle on my back feeling very heavy. Soon after this he fell out, and making sure I should find him in some corrie, plucked up heart and went on. Yes, there he was, but with his head well up, and apparently not very sick. Getting up, he limped to the top of the ridge, but not liking the look of the ground, turned back, and caught sight of me full in the open. After staring a minute, he cantered off quite strong, heading for a snow-ridge which ran along the top of the opposite sky-line, and fell away on this side in a steep curtain. He paused for a moment as he got near this obstacle, then putting on a spurt, he popped over and disappeared.

As there was an icy wind, sure forerunner of a snowstorm, and which froze the very marrow in my bones, I did not stop long to consider my position; and though disliking the idea of leaving a wounded animal, I felt that to follow it into an unknown region, in the midst of a snowstorm, would be madness. I therefore began to retrace my steps. The descent over rocky *débris* covered with snow was very laborious; even stout shooting-boots with nails gave a very uncertain grip, and a slip meant a sprained ankle or worse. After a time I got out of the snow-cloud, and could see my way better. The slope was still very rough, and my boots, of which I had not too many pairs, were getting cut to pieces. By degrees I got to the bottom of the ravine, and while thinking over my luck, and wondering what the others were doing, did not look about very much, but, on turning a corner, looked up the nullah, which was pretty steep, and there, to my astonishment, were seven gooljas, standing in single file, about 200 yards off. In a second my rifle was unslung, and before they had realised the situation I gave them one, two, right and left. Neither fell to the shot, but the leader seemed to stagger, took two strides down the slope, then recovered himself and followed the rest. Reloading, I gave him another shot, and down he went head over heels. Running after the others, I looked for blood-tracks, but finding none, though I followed within sight a good way, I gave in where they disappeared over a spur, and returned to where my ram lay. He had a good thick head, which measured, although broken off at the tips, 58 inches by 17 inches.

As it was getting late and I did not know how far off the camp lay, I rolled him down the slope into a deep water-course, and stuck my mountain-stick into the ground, with a red cotton handkerchief tied to it, to mark the spot and keep off the birds; then I started off across the steppe in the direction of the camp. When I got to the far edge of the plain, I found I had made a good shot, for there lay our camp at my feet, about two miles off. The prospect of food and drink freshened me considerably, and quickening my pace, I soon reached it. Bower and Dauvergne were still on the mountain.

The servants came crowding up with the usual anxious inquiry, " Kutch shikar mella ? "—" Have you had any sport ? " But I suddenly found I was dead beat, and could only reply, " Bring me tea at once!" Whilst I was going, I did not realise how done I was; but now, as I lay on my camp-bed, I came to the conclusion that I had never done such a hard day's work. Some tea soon revived me, and calling to Barat, I told him to send a pony to bring in the last goolja. He said the shikaris had not yet returned from the first beat, so I gave him directions to follow my track over the snow which covered the steppe, and he could not fail to see the red handkerchief on the opposite side; then changed my things, lit a pipe, and felt quite jolly again.

Bower and Dauvergne came in soon after, having seen plenty, but they had not killed any. Bower, who is as strong a walker as I ever met, was just as dead beat as I had been, and we came to the conclusion that, to work on these Pamir ranges, a good meal at starting is necessary. Walking on an empty stomach does not answer.

We had gone out in the early morning after a

ROUND THE TENT FIRE.

very light repast, and only a bit of bread in our pockets to last the day! I had never felt the altitudes farther south in Tibet or Ladak half so much as here, which, I fancy, is due to the cold being greater farther north, though our altitude to-day was not over 17,000 feet at the most.

We had a snug little dinner that evening in my tent, which was the largest of the three, and afterwards sat round a big fire made of a sort of peat, of which we found a fine deposit close to camp. This is formed by the droppings of sheep, which are always penned close together at night; and as the Kirghiz invariably camp on the same spot, it gradually accumulates, and being hardened and dried by the summer sun, when dug up into peats it forms excellent fuel. To make a good fire of it, it has to be built into a hollow cone open at the top. In the middle of this cone a heap of dry *burtsa* is placed. This burns fiercely for a bit, and sets alight the inside of the peats, whilst the air penetrates all round through the interstices. Once the pile is well alight, it throws out great heat, and never goes out until the whole is consumed. The only drawback to this style of firing is the smell of the smoke, which is horrible!

The following morning was lovely, not a cloud

to be seen. I was soon on the track of a herd of poli which were feeding on the plain, but from the lie of the ground it was impossible to stalk them, though it was not for want of trying, and I found I was only running a very good chance of being frost-bitten, so gave it up, and crossed to the spot where I had left the big poli the previous day. Not a trace of it remained, though Barat had only brought in the head and skin, leaving the body, which had not been made lawful food, according to Mussulman ideas, by having its throat cut. The wolves had been there during the night, and demolished every scrap. Nor could I make anything of the wounded one, though his tracks were visible until coming to stony ground, when all traces vanished.

A hearty breakfast and a pipe was a pleasant variety, and we agreed that hunting poli was the hardest work in the world, and it would be well to keep ourselves fresh for another day.

Dauvergne now bade us good-bye, and started on his return journey for Wakhan.

After toiling again all day unsuccessfully, we determined to try a new ground, and started down the main valley south-east from camp, towards the mouth of the Kilik valley, which ran down from the Kunjut border, taking a couple of yaks with us to bring back the spoils if we got any.

We had not gone very far on the steppe which ran along the edge of the valley when we saw some lammergeirs sitting about, which meant meat of some sort in the vicinity. Looking about, I thought there was a dead animal, and on drawing near found it to be a poli ram. A good deal had been eaten by the lammergeirs the previous day, and they were evidently waiting for the sun to thaw the meat, which had frozen hard during the night, to conclude their meal. We went on, wondering how he had met his death, when it suddenly struck me he must be the one I had wounded, and going back, I examined him more closely. I could not make out any bullet-wound, but one haunch amongst other parts had been eaten away; and as vultures always begin at a wounded spot, I came to the conclusion it was probably my ram, so told my yak-man to cut off its head,—a very fair one, measuring about 50 inches,—and bring it on.

The formation of this valley (the Kilik) was like all those of any size in these parts, having a steppe of undulating or flat ground on either side of the ravine through which the river cuts its way. The poli lie about on these steppes, where there is a certain sort of grass which springs up through the gravel; but in the early morning, or at night, they go down to the flats by the river, where they can feed with less trouble.

We sighted some gooljas, but they were out in the open, and unstalkable, and after hunting up the valley until within view of the glacier at its head, and having investigated all the likely ground, we retraced our steps to the mouth of the nullah, where we found my yak-man with the head of the poli, with which we returned.

My next chance was after a long and difficult stalk, finally having to scramble over the rocks as hard as I could go, so that I was not at all in a fit state to fire. On my getting up to them the herd stood for a moment, but it was a good 200 yards off. However, pulling myself together as well as I could in my breathless condition, I fired right and left. Clean misses both! Reloading, I gave them two more shots as they scrambled up the mountain-side. I watched them for some time, in hopes that one might be hit and fall out; but no such luck,—on they went, stopping every now and again to look back, and at last they disappeared over the top of the ridge. Smoking a pipe of bitterness, I wandered over the ground where my first ram was shot, but no Ovis had been about since my last visit, and turning back to camp, I found Bower in before me. He also had had a shot with no result.

In the evening a man arrived from Chaddirtash, the Kirghiz camp at the mouth of the valley, to say that news had come from the Little Pamir of Gromchefski, the Russian explorer, who had sent to let Kutch Mahomed, the Beg, know that he would probably be here in a day or two, on his way to Raskum, and wished to ascertain where we were camped, as he would like very much to meet us. Not knowing Russian, I wrote him a note in English, telling him where we were, and asking him to join us for a few days' shooting. I translated the gist of the note to the bearer, and told him to explain it to Gromchefski if he did not understand it.

To the non-sporting reader, if I have any, descriptions of our unsuccessful days' hunting may seem unnecessary; but if record only of good sport were given, the trials of the chase would be entirely overlooked, and a wrong impression conveyed. The hardships of the life, the fatigue which could scarcely be borne were it not for the hope of better luck which buoys every true hunter up, must to a certain extent be entered into to enable a real impression to be formed of the life we led. As a gambler lays his all on the throw of the dice, so does a hunter stake his hopes for the future, always with the firm belief that the next move will be the lucky one. And so we worked on in faith.

Going to the nullah where I had made my last shot and miss, I spotted a herd in a capital position, and hugged myself with the idea of an easy stalk. But not a bit of it. They left the nullah to graze in the open. There was nothing for it but to lie down and wait. The sun was getting up, which meant a change of wind, and if they did not move soon, my chance was gone. One by one they went towards a depression, and disappeared. As the last scut went out of sight, I got up and ran after them, but before getting to the edge, paused a moment to get my breath, when, horror of horrors! I felt the wind on my back. It was all up then, but I went on and looked over the brow. They had evidently got my wind, and had made their first rush, for they stood looking towards me. It was a long shot, and I was quite unsteady, but took the chance, threw up my rifle and fired. The bullet fell short into the snow. Giving a little more elevation, I tried the second barrel, but with no better success. So, after giving the nullah one more chance, and finding my friends comfortably settled, evidently for the day, with a fine extensive view all round, we agreed to change our ground, and gave orders to march the caravan down to the mouth of the Kilik.

Bower was to try the left side of the valley, and I started up towards the col, from Kukturuk. Here there were fresh tracks of a good herd of gooljas, but I got to the crest of the pass without seeing them. At the top of the col a rocky spur came down from the left, shutting out the view like a wall, and we (the shikari and myself) had to work our way round the end of it before we could see the snow-slopes above. There were the herd, busy digging up the snow to get at the grass.

As the wind is very shifty on these heights, we got back quickly, and made a detour to get well above them. It took an hour's hard walking, crossing a succession of rocky spurs from 10 to 20 feet in height. Climbing each one cautiously, we looked over the third, and there they were, quite twenty of them, about 150 yards off, looking grand on the white snow, and quite unsuspicious of our presence. Some were scraping holes in the snow, others lying down on the bare spots they had made.

As far as I could see, the best heads were farthest off, but I determined to take time and choose a real good one. While watching, one that had been lying down with some others in a clump got up and showed his horns clearly defined against the snow, as he turned his head and looked in my direction. I could resist no longer, and, drawing a steady bead on him, let drive. The bullet struck, not with that *thud* so dear to the sportsman's ear, but with a crack as if it had struck a rock. He appeared staggered for a moment, then shaking his head, made off with the rest of the herd down the slope as hard as they could pelt, never pausing for an instant. I took a running shot at another, which must have missed.

My feelings can be better imagined than described. My first inclination was to shie my empty rifle after them, my second to sit down and cry! I never felt so sick in my life. After having made such a beautiful stalk, and taken everything so quietly, only to succeed in hitting my game on the horn! Why had I not waited a moment longer? He was standing broadside on, but with his head turned towards me, and so covered his shoulder with his horn.

I watched them for a long time. Having ascended the hill on the opposite side, about half a mile from where I sat, they proceeded to cross a corrie, when all of a sudden they turned as if by word of command, and came scampering back! At the same moment I heard a rumbling, and saw the snow which had accumulated in the corrie begin to pour over the edge of the precipice, which fell away suddenly, just below where they were crossing. After running back some distance, they stopped as suddenly as they had started. My shikari made signs that we should follow them, as they were evidently frightened at the avalanche they had set in motion.

It did not take us long to run down; but when we began to ascend the opposite side, it was quite another thing. The slope lay at an angle of 45°, and the snow more than knee-deep in places.

We toiled and sobbed up the hill for half an

hour at least, while they stood gazing at the corrie, and I began to think they would wait for me after all; but whilst we were still a long way off, they made up their minds, and started again up the mountain-side.

Looking at each other in despair, we sorrowfully descended the slope the way we came, and then tried one of the branches of the Kilik, right up to the glacier at the head, but with no result. The day was getting on, so we turned about and made for camp.

Bower having fared no better, we decided to move to the mouth of the Mintaka, a valley leading down from the Kunjut border. Beyond getting a most magnificent view of snow-mountains in every direction, as far as eye could reach, we might have saved ourselves the scramble; so as we expected Gromchefski would by this time have arrived at Chaddirtash, we proceeded there, and were most hospitably received, and entertained by Kutch Mahomed with tea and a sort of girdle-cake, which the Kirghiz women made with flour, cream, and butter,—very acceptable to a hungry man.

The Russian not having come, we left the Karachunkar valley and turned up the Taghdumbash Pamir towards the Mustagh range, passing some groups of Sirikuli *yurts*. These people come on this pamir to graze their flocks in the summer, and in the winter return to the smaller villages in the lower part of the valleys.

Akal Jahn, the Beg of the neighbourhood, whose acquaintance we had already made on our journey up, entertained us, and told us where we were likely to find some gooljas, and also introduced two Kirghiz, the best shikaris, he said, in the country.

We walked up an easy road for about ten miles to the base of a broad col, the Kunjerat Pass, and there, sheltered by a circle of rocks, we made our camp. Bower and I started up this col together, and separated to the right and left. We had not gone far when I saw a herd of rams on the slopes on Bower's side, which he evidently saw also, and I watched him through the glasses manœuvring for a chance. Then, when about half-way across the plain, I sighted another herd, and made out some good heads. After making one or two false stalks, and having to wait and change my tactics as the wind veered round, I worked my way very carefully down. Instead of my double .500, I had brought out the Martini carbine, which had not yet shot an animal, and thought of giving it a turn. Having loaded, I crawled to the top of a hillock, and found the herd still lying down and half asleep. The moment I showed myself on the sky-line they were on their legs. I selected one, and gave him a shot which plugged into him, but did not bring him down, and he went on with the rest in single file. I got in another cartridge and fired again. This time they went round a swell, which covered them, and going after, I gave them two more shots, and thought I heard every bullet tell, but, as yet, none had fallen, so, sitting down, I watched them going along the bottom and up the opposite slope. Here one began to go short, turned along the side, and lay down behind a rock. Expecting that Bower on the heights above would meet the herd, and if the wounded ones lagged, turn them back to me, I hurried along, and on crossing the line of the herd found two distinct blood-tracks. Being anxious to follow, I went to the wounded one, and as he staggered up gave him another shot, and set off up the hill, along a rough track, which wound in and out the inequalities of the moraine, so that it was impossible to see far ahead. Just then there were two rapid shots above. Bower, then, had met the herd; but I did not feel easy about his having met the wounded ones, so kept on. The ground grew more and more rocky and broken, till it fell abruptly from the glacier into a deep ravine and brought me to a full stop. Presently, seeing Bower ascending the opposite side of the ravine to my left, I turned and went to the right; but after hunting for some time among the rocks, where the traces grew fainter and fainter, and beginning to feel I had done a good day's work, circled round to see about the dead ram, at which I had scarcely looked. As he lay on his side he appeared to have a very fair head, but on turning him over I found one horn was broken, which spoilt his beauty considerably.

Sitting down to smoke a pipe while the shikari cut off the head and skinned him, I soon felt better, and taking out my knife, began at the other end. We then quartered him, and hiding the meat and skin under some rocks, started for camp with the head slung on my mountain-pole, which we carried between us.

Bower came in soon after. He had made out the wounded ones, but could not get a chance at them; a long shot at two others had no results. The wounded one had a grand head, but he was going so strong that it was useless following. In the distance he saw another, not far from where I had my shots, looking very sick, and was quite surprised I had not found him. Later he had two more shots, and hit one hard, but as the day was getting on, faced about for home, expecting to find him under a rock on the morrow.

I was far from satisfied with my performance. Was it my fault, or the rifle? Out of four beasts, only one bagged; and I could not help thinking that had I used my double .500 this would not have occurred.

Starting off to seek dead, I got on the track in some snow, and could see the bullet had been through his body, there being blood on both sides of the track. Farther along there appeared fresh marks of wolves, and though knowing there was now no chance of his body, felt sure of finding his head; but though I searched high and low, not a trace was to be seen.

While sitting in my tent consoling myself with a cup of tea, Bower came in looking radiant. When following the ram wounded the previous day, a very fine goolja had started up suddenly within 100 yards of him, and paused a moment. Throwing up his rifle, which fortunately he had loaded in his hand, he dropped him before he could get away.

Going up the nullah next morning, which debouched near our camp from the north, I spotted a herd of ibex, and with my glasses made out two bucks amongst them, but as their horns were small, let them be. Five miles farther on, the nullah took a bend, and on rounding the shoulder a most magnificent view greeted me.

I was looking into a kind of amphitheatre. The rocky precipices which bound it were too steep for snow to lodge on, and for this reason had formed a huge glacier at the base. Out of this glacier, which ended in a wall of ice at least 300 feet high, sprang the stream, one of the sources of the Tashkurgan river. It was superb, but impassable, — so turned back, and indulged in a square meal in camp for a change.

Bower had great good-luck, having come suddenly on another herd of Ovis, and dropped three. Luckily he had ponies with him to collect the spoils of the previous day. It was dusk before they got in with their load. The largest head measured 60 inches, the finest we had shot; the others were not very big.

A messenger coming in to say that Gromchefski had arrived at Chaddirtash, we mounted our ponies and started for Akul Jahn's camp. He was not at home, having gone to meet Younghusband, who was exploring all the passes of the Mustagh range.

As the pamir is quite flat here, we could make out in the distance the *mazar*, where we expected to find the camp, but could see no signs of it. Presently we met some Kirghiz who had been sent to conduct us thither, and who said it was no distance; but, like the Scotch " mile and a bittock," the "bittock" was the longest part, and we travelled a good six miles before we reached our destination.

Gromchefski had only just arrived, but soon got a small tent up, and offered us tea and biscuits. He had with him a German, whose name has escaped me. Our conversation was rather curious. I talked French, but understood German a little. Gromchefski talked German, but understood a little French! I therefore addressed him in French, and he replied in German. He was travelling, he said, for the Russian Geographical Society; but his real work was at Marghilan, where he held a post similar to our Assistant Commissioner, and had got leave of absence to travel and explore the frontier. He was anxious to know if the authorities at Leh would let him through without a passport. So I told him, if he went as a private individual they would, but if he marched in with his Cossacks in full uniform, a great deal of correspondence between our relative Governments would have to be gone through before leave could be sanctioned.

We sat for an hour or two, and then, though loath to leave, were obliged to make a start, as daylight was ebbing fast.

CHAPTER VI.

JOURNEY TO YARKAND.

A CHANGE OF LATITUDE—FISHING—A DAY WITH YOUNGHUS-
BAND—*EN ROUTE* FOR YARKAND—TAGHERMA PEAK—SUF-
FERINGS OF THE PONIES — RUFUS SUCCUMBS — AN AWK-
WARD GORGE—ACROSS THE TORAK TO THE CHARLUNG
VALLEY—CLIMBING A PRECIPICE—THE KARA AND THE
KIZIL DAWAN—AN ICY ROAD—MIDNIGHT BREAKFAST—A
LONG TRAMP—THE FORT AT LAST.

It being now the middle of October and the cold rapidly becoming greater, we felt it was time to move to a lower region, so determined to have a try for the *bōghe*, or maral stag, on the banks of the Zarafshan beyond Yarkand.

The streams that we had forded a few days previously were already frozen so hard that the ponies could walk on the ice; and Barat said that the passes we had to cross beyond Tashkurgan would very shortly be snowed up, and travelling consequently very unpleasant.

Our way lay down by the *mazar*[1] to Tashkurgan, where we found what was to us luxury and civilisation, after our sojourn in the upper regions of the Taghdumbash.

A note came to us in the evening from Major Younghusband, who was a great friend of Bower's, saying he would leave his camp, which was near the *mazar*, and take a run down to see us.

There were some hot springs, a native told me, where fish were to be found as long as my arm; so, thinking I might as well employ the spare time, I got out my rod. I tried a fly, then a spoon, but they would have neither, so chanced my last resource, a single hook with a shot on it, baited with a bit of raw meat. I lay down on the bank above a shoal of fish that reposed in a nice pool with about 6 feet of water, and watched my bait float gradually down on to the nose of the leading fish: the water was so clear that I saw him open his mouth and suck it in. He played well, but as there were weed-patches about, I did not give him much law, and soon had him out,—a nice-shaped fish of about 4 lb. weight, something between a

[1] *Mazar*—cairn of stones on which are piled the horns of Ovis, ibex, &c.

carp and a barbel, and which proved to be very fair eating. In this way I got eight fish, whose combined weight was 16 lb.

The change of climate was delightful after the intense cold, although we were still at an altitude of 10,000 feet, and at night the thermometer fell below zero, but during the day, when the sun was up, it rose as high as 75°.

The following day Younghusband arrived, having travelled on trotting camels furnished by Akal Jahn, which, he said, were first-rate conveyances—not very fast, but keeping up a steady pace of from four to five miles an hour for a long period.

We had a great "buck," as we call a long talk in India, and heard a certain amount of news, as he had left Leh after us, and had had mails forwarded. His intention was to explore the Kunjerat, where we had shot last, the Kukturuk valley, and over the Mintaka Dawan into Kunjut, and so back to Kashmir.

We spent another day together, and I fished the pools once more: the fish were getting shyer, but I landed a dozen of them, in all 22 lb. Then, bidding Younghusband farewell, we started towards Yarkand on October the 30th.

Going along the valley of the Tashkurgan river, we got into a very narrow gorge, with precipitous cliffs and slopes on each side. A range of mountains, called the Karatagh, spring from the Mustagh range on the south-west, and, running in a north-western direction, bind the Taghdumbash Pamir and this valley.

We had crossed this range, when we entered the district, at a comparatively low part, about 14,000 feet. After this they gradually rise, and culminate in the Tagherma Peak, which is reckoned at 25,000 feet!

About ten miles below Tashkurgan the vale, if I may so call it, ceases, and the river enters into this narrow gorge, where it seems to have cut its way right through the range. We had hoped to have followed the river, and so avoided crossing more passes; but this, we heard, was impossible, the gorge in many places being sheer down to the rocky bed of the river.

Three short marches brought us to what we thought to be the top of the pass, but when there we found a sort of convex table-land or pamir. When we got out of the ravine on to this pamir a very fine view lay before us. The plateau, about 144 miles in area, was freshly covered with snow, and surrounded by snow-covered peaks ascending tier upon tier to the great Tagherma Peak, already mentioned.

When we reached the centre of the plateau the path was well marked in the snow by a caravan of yaks, but as we began to descend the road became more difficult, owing to drifts of snow in the hollows and ravines which covered the track. The ponies commenced to struggle, and floundered into these drifts, and we had to flounder after them, take up their loads and readjust them! The altitude being high, the poor animals were incapable of much exertion, and we had often great difficulty in moving them. To add to our trouble, it came on to snow—not good, respectable, feathery snow, but nasty little particles of ice, which, drifting with the wind, nearly blinded us, and cut our faces severely. It was five o'clock before we got out of the snow-region, and dusk before we came to a small spring on a grass plot, near which was—oh, most welcome sight!—the wherewithal to cook our dinner, that useful article known in Switzerland as the *bois de vache!* Some of the ponies were late in arriving, and one, alas! —poor Rufus, as we called him, who had already distinguished himself by his fall over the *cud—*

never appeared at all. Barat, who always did rear-guard, said he came down once or twice, then fell for good and all. Poor beast! he tried to get on his legs, then gave it up, and lay still. Barat cut his nostril, but no blood came, and after a few minutes he stretched out his legs and died. This test of bleeding in one of the nostrils is always practised when ponies are overcome by exertion at high altitudes. It is considered infallible, both as a restorative if the blood flows, relieving the head, and as a sure sign that the case is hopeless if the blood does not flow.

We had not got over the worst, however, for the road next day was no better than the bed of a river, precipitous cliffs on each side, huge boulders and fallen rocks. The stream here and there was frozen and the rocks covered with a coating of ice! It was terrible work: every one had to go into the ice-cold water, and bodily lift not only the loads, but even the ponies, over bad places. Our loads were soaking wet; and when at last we got out of this fearful gorge, we thought ourselves fortunate to get all our animals in alive. It took us ten hours to journey five miles.

The next pass was the Torak, about 13,000

feet, an easy ascent and good road. We passed a herd of ponies on our way, and the next morning several of ours were absent without leave. We had to hunt the nullah for some time to find them, and at last got all but my riding-pony, Bob. We were just starting when he turned up, not looking a bit ashamed of himself, though he had evidently made a night of it with the herd we had seen on our way.

We now got down to grass prairie-land, with Kirghiz hamlets here and there. These were huts built of mud and stone. In this they are unlike their brethren of the Pamir, who scorn to live in anything but *yurts*.

Coming to the Charlung valley, we camped in a grove of apricot-trees belonging to a friend of Barat's, who very kindly brought us some fowls and *three* eggs, which, he said, were all that remained in the village. We had a great consultation as to what was to be done with the three eggs. One egg was a bad thing to split, so we decided on an omelette for breakfast. What is an egg, do you say? Please, kind reader, remember that we had eaten our last egg in August, and this was November! Barat's friend also brought us some beautiful rock-salt, in veins as white as snow, and perfectly free from grit. There was plenty of it, he said, a little way up the mountain behind the village.

After descending the valley some distance we entered a small ravine which looked like a *cul de sac*, for we soon found ourselves at the base of a cliff 300 feet high. At first we could see no way up, but Barat pointed out a tortuous path which wound up through clefts and crevices. He said we must unload and carry everything up bit by bit, and that the ponies would have to be shoved and hauled up as best we could! It certainly did look a nasty place, and various remains of deceased ponies lying about at the base did not afford us much encouragement. By dint of hard labour we at last got everything up to the shelf above the precipice, but not before dark, when the ponies, seeming to realise the situation, did their best.

Our way lay over the Kara Dawan, or black pass, so called from the colour of the formation of which it is composed; and then we turned up a ravine towards the Kizil Dawan, or red pass.

It was a long "travel," but during the day we

had an agreeable surprise. A Yarkandi whom we met, dismounted, and coming to me, asked my name. On hearing it he told me he had been sent by Mahomed Unis, the Badakshani Aksakal, with a packet of letters which had arrived by caravan. This was a real treat, for we had had no letters since we left Leh.

The Kizil Dawan was our final fence, and we had now a straight run before us; but although we were at a much lower altitude, 7000 feet, the night was the coldest we had experienced since we left the high Pamir. The thermometer went down to 3° below zero.

Our road went through one of the finest gorges I ever saw. The stream which we followed flowed between two tremendous cliffs, which rose up on each side for 400 feet: in places they were only 20 feet apart, and here and there they almost met overhead. It would have made a grand entrance to Gustave Doré's "Inferno." The water was frozen, and we had to cross and recross every 20 yards or so. Sometimes it bore the ponies, but in places they went through: the uncertainty made it very nasty travelling. Where the ice was very smooth and slippery we had to throw sand and gravel across. Of course, every now and again a pony, in sheer "cussedness," would leave the path made for them in this way, and perform a spread eagle on the ice!

On passing through the portals of this gorge we found ourselves in an open valley. Some Kirghiz women, who were cutting blocks of ice out of the frozen stream, told us that there was no water below this point at this season, except a few pools, which were so salt as to be unfit for use. This decided our camping, as for forty miles there was neither grass nor water,—a bad look-out for ponies in the condition ours were reduced to. However, Barat said he had done it before, and we should get through all right if we started at twelve o'clock at night.

A caravan of camels coming in from Yarkand, we went over to see them, and found they were carrying rice, dried apricots, and peaches, to trade with the Kirghiz in the neighbourhood. They had been going from five o'clock of the previous afternoon until 2 P.M., and said it was a terrible long march to the *karaol*.

As soon as the sun went down it became very cold, at which we were surprised, having expected a pleasant change in the temperature; but the natives explained that it was on account of what they call *shore*, which appears to be a mixture of salt and saltpetre, which exudes from the ground at the base of the mountains.

Getting up at midnight, we breakfasted (if a meal at that unholy hour can so be called) and made a start. It was cold and dark, and no moon to cheer us on our way. For fear of losing the road, we had to keep with the caravan, and tramped along in a mechanical sort of way. I got on my pony for a change, but found it too cold to ride. At about eight o'clock we came to a plain—the plain of Eastern Turkistan—when the long-wished-for sun rose, but it appeared through a mist, just as it does in a London fog! This was a sore disappointment, for we had looked forward to getting on our ponies as it grew warmer. Vain hope! The sun got higher and higher; but for all the good it was to us in the way of warmth, it might just as well have not been there at all. There was nothing for it but to tramp on to the end. Had we found fuel and water, we might have warmed ourselves with a hot meal; but as it was, frozen tea out of a bottle, and hard cold mutton, were not conducive to much caloric.

The ponies kept on at the same pace, and the

mist lifting a little at mid-day, we caught sight of a mud-fort across the plain, which was the *karaol*, or outpost, of Yarkand. It looked much nearer than it really was. Sometimes, as we descended into an imperceptible undulation in the plain, it disappeared altogether, and when we again came in sight it looked just as far off as ever.

At last we found ourselves on the edge of a steppe, and, as if a stage curtain had been raised by magic, a new scene lay before us. At our feet ran a broad canal, crossed by a good solid wooden bridge, and in front of it rose the fort, which had been appearing and vanishing so often like a Will-o'-the-wisp. The whole country as far as eye could reach was dotted with villages, clumps of trees, and orchards, and instead of the stony desert plain on which we stood, irrigated fields everywhere met the eye. They were, of course, quite bare at this time of year, but even so they were a pleasing variety.

As we approached the fort, some Turkis came running out, and catching hold of our bridles—for we had mounted our ponies in order to make our entry in due form—led us into the fort, and conducting us to a little hut, said we were to put up there and be their guests during our stay.

It was a very small apartment, but clean, and spread with *mundas*. There was a nice wood-fire blazing in an open hearth, which, rough as it looked, worked capitally, and did not smoke at all. On one side of the fireplace was a sort of platform, about a foot or so above the ground: on this *mundas* were also spread. This was the sleeping-place affected by the Turkis, and it made a capital lounge.

In a very short time, after a cup of tea and a toast at the fire, we felt like giants refreshed—so much so, that Bower said he would go and shoot some ducks, of which we had seen a good many on the canal. Feeling lazy in front of the good fire, and not at all bloodthirsty, I remained where I was. After resting a while I took a look round the inside of the fort, and had a talk with the Karaolchee, as the man in charge is called. He said that since the days of Yakub Beg these *karaols* had all been neglected, and some even destroyed by the Chinese. This one, for instance, whose interior area was 7000 square yards, only contained half-a-dozen huts similar to the one in which we were; the rest were in ruins. They seem to consider these forts of no value; and this road had very little traffic,—only an occasional caravan, such as we had met trading with the Kirghiz in the lower Tagherma valley, came that way. The road was considered so bad that the caravans to Tashkurgan and Badakshan from Yarkand all went by a longer but better route.

Bower returned with some fine mallard and pochards—a welcome addition to our larder; but he said he had some difficulty retrieving them when shot, as they flew up and down the canal, and he did not feel inclined to swim after them! We turned in early and slept the sleep of the just.

Our road took us through a well-cultivated country. The hamlets looked far cleaner and better built than the villages of India. The cottages varied a good deal in size and shape: the rooms were all very similar, each having a raised bedplace, and nice open fireplace which seldom smoked; and as the chimneys were short, this showed considerable engineering skill on the part of the constructor, although a Scotch mason will tell you that this is purely a matter of luck! Here and there in the fields we saw "coolen" (*Grus cinerea*) of India, wild ducks on every bit of water, while sand-grouse, very like the pin-tailed species of India, flew overhead; and Waffles and Joker started hares frequently, much redder and smaller than the mountain hares we had previously seen.

We were again the guest of an old Turki for the night. It is the universal custom in Turkistan that whoever puts you up supplies all you require; and on leaving, a present of some cotton print, a turban, or a few handkerchiefs is made, according to the value of the things supplied. As a rule they do not care for coin, except in caravanserais, which are constructed for the use of travellers on payment.

In the course of the day our Jiggit, or letter-carrier, whom we had sent to announce our arrival to Mahomed Unis at Yarkand, returned, bringing a sack full of melons, grapes, peaches, apples, and bread, sent by the Aksakal for our delectation. He asked for a note of acknowledgment, as he wished to return at once, saying eighty miles in two days was nothing to him or his pony.

CHAPTER VII.

YARKAND.

A TURKI'S HUT — OUR VILLA RESIDENCE — AN AWKWARD SITUATION—VISITING THE AMBAN—MAHOMED UNIS MAKES US A PRESENT—THE RETURN CALL—REFITTING.

YANGI-SHAHAR, or Chinese town of Yarkand, appeared, on approaching, to be a great square fort with high mud parapet and ditch. At intervals along the top of the parapet were loopholed towers, with the graceful concave sloping roofs and ornamental eaves so affected by the Chinese. There were embrasures along the parapet, but no guns appeared to be mounted. As we rode up to the gate of the city which opens northward on to the Kashgar road, a group of horsemen appeared, and dismounting, advanced to meet us. We concluded they must be Mahomed Unis and the Kashmiri Aksakal.

According to the custom of the country, we also dismounted and walked towards them. Shaking hands all round, we begged them to remount, and doing the same, asked them to conduct us to our place of residence, which we had begged might be outside the city walls.

Mahomed Unis, a particularly gentlemanly nice-looking man, was handsomely dressed in a cloth *choga*, with the high boots of the country (a sort of blucher-boot, made without a sole, like a moccasin; over this is worn a high-heeled slipper, which is kicked off on entering a room), and a white muslin turban very neatly put on. His manner was particularly good, and we took a great fancy to him at once. The Kashmiri Aksakal had only recently been raised to that post, and though he seemed a very good sort of man, did not show the same breeding and manner as the other. He was dressed in the same way. The rest of the party consisted of attendants, two of whom spoke Hindustani; and these, we were given to understand, were placed at our disposal during our stay at Yarkand, and would do whatever we told them. They conducted us round the city walls, until we came to the old or Turki city of Yarkand, passing the old Yangi Hissar of Yakub Beg on our right. This had been demolished by the Chinese, for no earthly reason except the love of destruction, as they built this city on similar ground close by.

In a suburb of gardens and orchards we were shown our place of abode. They feared we might find it cold, as it was built for a summer residence, but as we had asked to be without the city, it was the best they could do for us. It was a curious rambling building of bricks, composed more of verandahs fronted with lattice-work, rather than rooms, doubtless very pleasant in summer: but as we had asked for a country residence, we had to make the best of it; and we saw that by pasting up the lattice-work with thick paper, and keeping up good fires, we should do very well. There was plenty of wood, and they promised we should have an ample supply.

As soon as our ponies came in, we began to get our residence in order. A man was sent off for thick country paper and paste-pot, fires were lit, and in no time we had everything snug and ship-shape.

Visitors began to pour in, and the teapot

was in full swing—for afternoon and even morning tea is *de rigueur* in Turkistan. After seeing us settled, Mahomed Unis asked leave to depart, saying he would like to take my passport to the Amban and report our arrival in due form. I gave it, with my compliments to the great man, upon whom we would call on the morrow, if he would receive us. We then cleared the room of visitors, begging them to excuse our apparent rudeness, but we were going to have our midday meal, and should be glad to see them at some future time. Having got rid of our visitors and had some lunch, we began to realise that the first period of our wanderings was over, and that we must settle operations for the future, lay in supplies, refit generally, and buy or hire a new team of ponies.

Then came the question as to Bower's movements. By the mail that met us on the road he had received a letter from the Joint-Commissioner at Leh, asking him to undertake the hunt of Dad Mahomed, the murderer of Dalgleish, and for this purpose had sent him two men who knew the language of the country, and also funds to defray expenses, but, unfortunately, no passport. As he was travelling on mine, he did not see how he was to get on at all, unless the Amban of Yarkand would give him one. The situation was extremely awkward, as I had been instructed by the Minister at Pekin to be very careful while in the country, and to show that I was travelling for my own pleasure and in no way doing any political work. The arrival of the moonshi and jemadar from Leh might arouse suspicions, and it was impossible for Bower to explain to the Amban that he had simply come to catch Dad Mahomed, as the murderer was at large, and had friends among the Pathan merchants in most of the towns, who would at once give him notice if it transpired what he was after. His whereabouts was not known, reports being of the vaguest: some said Russian Turkistan, and others Kalmutz on the frontiers of China. Altogether, we thought it rather a wild-goose chase; but, having undertaken it, Bower said he would try his best. I, on the other hand, had come to shoot, and did not intend to waste my time. Bower decided that, failing the Amban, he would go to the Dotai, or governor, of Kashgaria, explain the matter to him, and ask for a passport; whilst I proceeded by the

I

Yarkand river to the Maralbashi, to hunt for the maral stag in the forests which covered its banks. On the morrow, when we called on the Amban, we would explain that, though we had hitherto travelled together, Bower wished to see Kashgar and its neighbourhood, whilst I was anxious to prosecute my search for natural history specimens, for which business, as my passport showed, I had come to the country, and that Bower would return and meet me at Maralbashi; after which we could act as circumstances required.

The following day we put on our best clothes to do honour to the governor. Mahomed Unis suggested we should pass through the city and bazaars, as it was market-day, and we should see them in full swing.

After riding about a mile we entered the city by the west gate, and found ourselves suddenly plunged into a regular vortex: ponies laden, ponies ridden, donkey-carts, men, women, and children, filled the streets and lanes, people selling and people buying, loafers and beggars; in one place a story-teller, telling tales of love and war; in another a Mullah holding forth at the top of his voice, preaching the tenets of

Islam, and denouncing all those who did not follow the Prophet, to eternal perdition.

The shops or stalls which lined the way exposed all sorts of wares: in some, cottons, prints, and bright-coloured handkerchiefs from Manchester; in others, gorgeous *chogas* and silks from Khotan and Andigan in Russian Turkistan. Then there were furriers selling furs, *poshteens*, and the huge otter-skin hats which the women wear, boot-shops, fruit-shops, shops of cheap Birmingham hardware goods, butchers, bakers, and confectioners. After the solitude of the Pamir the bustle made us feel quite giddy.

From the north gate we crossed the bridge over the ditch which surrounds the fortified Yangi Hissar, and found ourselves in the Chinese quarters. Here the same scene met our eyes. We had expected to find nothing but Chinamen; but with the exception of a few mixing with the crowd of Turkis, and some keeping shops, there was nothing to distinguish one quarter from another, except that the shops were perhaps better built, and the main street broader than the one in the old city.

About a quarter of a mile up the street we turned into a large courtyard through a pair of very imposing gates, and found ourselves in front of others gorgeously painted and decorated. This, we were told, was the entrance of the *yaman*, and here we must dismount. After some parley between Mahomed Unis and the Chinese officials, we were shown into a little anteroom to wait till the Amban returned from his drive. We were given some very weak tasteless tea, and a curious sort of water-pipe, much affected by the Chinese. As I did not understand this article, I took a good pull at it, filling my mouth with dirty water, which I promptly spat out, much to the amusement of the Chinese attendants. Just at this moment a Chinaman ran in, and announced that the Amban was ready. We were shown out past the gates we had noticed on our entry, on the other side of which we saw the great man standing prepared to receive us.

Now I had heard that the amount of honour done to a visitor by a Chinese official is shown by the number of gates opened for him on his reception, so that I did not like this side entry at all; but as he stood waiting, there was nothing for it but to move on to greet him. He shook us both by the hand, and by signs waived us before him into a reception-hall. Here the big doors were opened all right, and we were conducted to a raised platform in the centre of the room, on which were two chairs of sorts, with a table between them, which we found afterwards was so placed for the ceremony of drinking tea. Having shown us to our seats, the Amban took his in a sort of side aisle; but the conversation being carried on at third hand, our Hindustani translating into Turki and the Turki again into Chinese, it did not progress rapidly.

The Amban said he hoped we had not suffered from the length and hardships of our journey, and that we found ourselves comfortable in Yarkand. We replied that all the trouble and fatigue of the journey was amply repaid by the pleasure of arriving at such a charming spot, where every one, and he especially, was so good to us. Then came the usual questions as to the reason for our journey. Next, for what purpose we shot animals: was it to make medicine of their horns or bones? When we told him we stuffed and preserved the heads, he said he supposed we put them up to worship as idols! and on our replying that we did in a sort of way, he seemed satisfied, and asked if we were afraid to kill tigers. On saying that, on the contrary, we hoped for an opportunity, as we should take the skin home, he inquired if we kept the bones, and on hearing they were no good to us, begged that we would send them to him, as they were much prized to make medicine of. He said they also used the horns of the maral stag for this purpose, but to be of any use they must be procured in summer, when they are soft in velvet.

We now, according to regulation, asked permission to drink a cup of tea which had been placed at our elbow on first entry. The Chinese way of drinking tea is to put the leaf into a cup, fill it up with hot water, and let it draw before drinking. It is served to visitors in a cup of honour—*i.e.*, a cup standing in a square saucer, with a round one covering the top. With very great men the under saucer is made of silver.

After explaining our reasons for parting from one another, we asked if he could not give Bower a separate passport. He said this was not feasible, as he was inferior in rank to the Dotai or governor, and that we had better go on to Maralbashi together, and Bower might then go on to Kashgar. There was nothing further to be done, so we took our leave, and he very graciously conducted us to our ponies in the outside yard. This time the great gates were opened for our egress.

When we got outside, Mahomed Unis asked if we would do him the great honour of a visit. We said nothing would give us greater pleasure; and also told the Kashmiri Aksakal that we would visit him if he would permit us, which seemed to please him, and he went off to get his place ready for our reception.

We found Mahomed Unis's dwelling very nice and comfortable. Like most of the better-class houses of this neighbourhood, it had two or three good-sized, fairly lofty rooms opening on a square yard, enclosed by a high wall and entered by a big gate. The larger the gate the more importance it gives the dwelling. This idea is, I fancy, borrowed from the Chinese. On nearing the house, Mahomed Unis asked leave to go on to prepare for our reception; and when we rode up he came out and conducted us through, taking my pony by the bridle. This is a point of etiquette with the Turkis. You then dismount, and are led into the house. In a very roomy apartment, well carpeted with *mundas*, a *dusterkhan* was laid out on a low table before the fireplace. It consisted of cakes, fruit, almonds, raisins, &c. He begged us to do him the honour of partaking of his humble fare. Saying we had not seen such a good spread for a long time, we endeavoured to do justice to it. The same formalities had to be gone through at the Kashmiri Aksakal's.

Mahomed Unis said that he had a great wish to present us each with a pony, for we had been consigned to his charge, and that for very shame he must provide us with one apiece. We represented that such a thing could not be—that we had ponies already; but he looked so disappointed at our refusal, that we had to give in at last and accept his generous offer.

When we got back to our own house we found a lot of visitors waiting our return, so had to do tea again for the fourth time! By the evening, when at last we got rid of them, we felt quite knocked up, having had to keep up a strained conversation of polite phrases and nonsense for the greater part of the day.

The following morning the Amban returned our visit. We had arranged a sort of audience-hall for his reception; and after sitting about twenty minutes, he took his departure. We conducted him out, and handed him to his carriage,—a two-wheeled conveyance, with a top to it, drawn by a mule.

In the evening the Amban's Tunktchi, or interpreter, arrived, bringing us a present of flour, rice, sheep, wood, &c. Giving the pony-men some red cloth and a few rupees for their trouble, we next day sent the Amban a watch in return. We also tried to induce Mahomed Unis to take one, but in vain. He said he did not understand it, and should not be able to make it go.

Meanwhile the process of refitting was being got through. As can be imagined, after the amount of walking, our boots and *chuplies*[1] were pretty well done for—indeed I had only one pair of shooting-boots fit to wear, and my *chuplies* were all in holes. We were obliged to provide ourselves with the *charoks* or shoes of the country, which are made of goat-leather, the sole being of cow's skin. When the leather is wet, it is put on a mould, and modelled something after the shape of a slipper; but there is no fit about them, and they look like a great walnut-shell. The upper leather is slit down to the instep, and a tape passed through a loop

---

[1] *Chuplies*, or sandals, worn in Kashmir with a leather sock, excellent for lightness, but which soon wear out on rough ground.

above the heel ties them on. They are worn over a high stocking made of felt, and are very warm and comfortable; but if your feet are not pretty hard in the soles, you feel the stones very much, as there is only a single bit of leather, and that not of the thickest, between you and the ground. The great drawback to them is, that the leather is badly tanned and very rotten, and therefore lasts no time.

Bower continued his endeavour to get a passport from the Amban, but without success; so I agreed to let him have mine, on condition that he should either send or bring it himself to Maralbashi.

After going over the *pros* and *cons* between buying or hiring a team of ponies, I decided on the latter, and got them from Mahomed Unis—a decision I never had cause to regret. My team consisted of eight ponies for my own use, and three spare ones for the service of the caravan.

A man called Mahomed Atta, a Badakshi, who proved an excellent servant, and who spoke a little Hindustani, was in charge, with a couple of drivers under him. I also took on one of the men that had come with us from Kashmir in

Barat's service, Rahamut by name, to look after my own riding-ponies. He was a very good servant, and knew sufficient Hindustani for us to be able to understand each other. Having settled this, and got *charoks* and *poshteens* (a loose coat of dressed sheepskin, worn with the woolly side in), also rugs of the same to sleep under, and various stores and little luxuries for the road, I laid in, besides, a supply of *gamboos*, a Chinese coin, simply a lump of solid silver made in a rough mould, valued, according to its weight, from ten rupees to a hundred and fifty; *darchen*, a copper Chinese coin, about half the size of a halfpenny, with a square hole cut in the middle —these are strung together in a double row, 500 in all, worth about five rupees; *tillas*, a gold coin of the time of Yakub Beg, value about five rupees — they are larger but thinner than a half sovereign; the little silver *tonga*, five of which go to a rupee, and which are now nearly obsolete, another relic of Yakub Beg's time; and finally, a large bundle of piece-goods, for presents to the natives.

CHAPTER VIII.

FROM YARKAND TO AKSU.

TOUCHING FAREWELLS—BOWER TAKES ANOTHER ROUTE—ON THE ROAD TO MARALBASHI — A FALCON PARTY—HOSPITABLE VILLAGERS—A FOREST OF THE PAST—SHOOTING JERAN—A MUSICAL TURKI SPOILS SPORT—A FALSE ALARM—VISITED BY A CHINAMAN—A FINE STAG—THE YANGI HISSAR—A CARAVANSERAI—TIGERS—A MESSAGE FROM BOWER—CHILLON—MARCH TO AKSU—MAHOMED AMIN—A WELCOME *NAZAR*—THE TIAN SHAN MOUNTAINS—AN EXCITING GALLOP—CURIOUS HUTS—WILD CAMEL.

As there was what is called a good road to Kashgar, Bower engaged an *araba*, or country cart, with a top to it. It had two wheels, each 6 feet in diameter, one horse in the shafts, and a pair, sometimes three, in the lead. We were astonished at what we considered the unnecessary length of traces, rather more than a horse's length from nose to tail, of the leaders; but once on the road, this was soon explained. It was so rough and uneven that the leaders were often on one path and the wheeler on another —in fact, had to go all over the place as best they could.

In parting with Mahomed Unis and the Kashmiri Aksakal, we presented each with a robe of honour of good English broadcloth, placing it, after the Eastern custom, on their shoulders, which piece of attention pleased them greatly. We felt very grateful to these good people for all their civility, and wished we could have given them some adequate return in the way of a present. Money we could not give, for fear of offending them.

After many touching farewells, Bower and I started, going together as far as the first stage on the road to Maralbashi. Here we parted on the 25th of November.

My way lay through a cultivated country irrigated by canals, with hamlets and orchards dotted about. The first curiosity were the milestones, which are found on all the main roads. These consist of pyramids of mud bricks 20 feet high, which are placed about two and a half miles apart. As it struck me that the intervals varied a good deal, I inquired the reason, and was told that it was on account of the difficulty there was in some parts in getting water to make the bricks of which they were constructed. This was considered quite a sufficient reason in Turki eyes!

My first halt was at a village called Terrek Langar, and my guide found a mud hovel, about 10 feet square, which was to be my domicile, out of which we first had to eject some goats. It was certainly not very pretentious, but answered my purpose well enough, having the usual little fireplace, where a blaze soon made things cheery; and I thoroughly enjoyed a quiet evening, after the perpetual fuss and bother of Yarkand.

The ponies worked admirably, and did their eighteen miles in five hours. So far the country was open—here and there tracks of sandhills, and low scrub jungle, out of which we put up some pheasants.

We came upon a party of natives mounted on ponies, some of them having big brown eagles on their wrists, hooded and jessed like the ordinary falcon. They told me they were going to hunt the jeran antelope. I should have much liked to join them, but having a twenty-mile march before me, could not spare the time.

THE COUNTRY PEOPLE. 143

The jungle improved in size and growth as we got farther on. Formerly the forest had extended to Yarkand, but in course of years it had been cleared for timber and firewood.

I took a great fancy to the country people, and found them very much nicer than those in the towns, who were independent and grasping, while with the villagers some cotton print and a few handkerchiefs were always received with delight, and were the only things the hospitable souls would accept. On entering a village they would just look at you, and wonder who you were, and did not bother you as they did in the towns, where the Chinamen would hop up to you like a jackdaw, and after looking you over, begin to pull about your things, now and again making a remark in an abrupt impertinent way. They will walk into your room without knocking, examine your property, and even take the pipe out of your mouth and have a pull at it! This, I was told, was rather a sign of goodwill than otherwise.

Chinese Turkistan is filled with the scum of the Chinese population, as, excepting the officials, who are not amiss, the small traders and soldiers are all criminals and bad characters of sorts, who are offered the alternative of a prison in China or service in Turkistan. There is, in spite of all his faults, one good point in the Chinese character: however low a man may be in the social scale, he manages to dress himself respectably. No doubt his person and habits are very dirty, and he stinks like a badger; still, he presents a tidy exterior. They are a miserable race as to size, and although they look wretched, seldom ail, which is a proof of the saying, "A Chinaman is only ill once in his life, and that when he dies." The soldiers are miserable specimens, and the officers either drunk or insensible from opium. Their towns are fortified, and surrounded by good brick parapets and ditches, but no guns mounted — indeed I do not believe they have any in this country.

At this point of the journey my guide missed the way, but the country being open, we struck across the jungle which separated us from the road, and came upon the most extraordinary forest, consisting of large trees of the aspen and poplar species, which predominate in this region. But it was a forest of the past: not a weed or a blade of grass was alive. The soil was fine dust mixed with *shore*, slightly crusted on the top, though not sufficient to bear the weight of the ponies, who sank into it over their hocks. The trunks of the trees, which were from 20 to 30 yards apart, were half buried in the soil, evidently the deposit of dust-storms from the great Gobi Steppe in the south. This, I fancy, had choked them, and there they stood, assuming a more and more weird fantastic appearance in the gradual course of decay. Simply a skeleton forest—a splendid study of utter desolation for an artist's brush.

At Aksak Maral the Beg very civilly called, and promised to find me shikaris who knew their way about. There were, he said, jeran antelope not far off.

The morning was intensely cold, and when I went out a thick hoar-frost hung on the trees and grass, and my hands became so numbed that I hoped the sun would rise before having a chance of a shot.

We came across the slots of deer—first a herd of hinds or maral, and after, on that of a solitary *bōghe*, or stag,—they appeared narrower and smaller than those of the barasingh in Kashmir, or even of our own red deer; and in the sand there were the pugs of a large tiger, quite fresh: these I followed until they led into the high grass.

After wandering about I caught sight of something moving in the grass, and with the aid of the glass made it out to be a jeran, but a doe: however, as I wanted a specimen for the skin, I set to work to stalk it—no easy matter, their senses being wonderfully keen. The grass getting too short to cover me, I put up the 200 sight of my rifle and took a careful steady shot: the bullet told, and after turning a couple of somersaults the jeran lay still. It was a full-grown doe, in actual size not much bigger than the gazelle of India, but the length and thickness of its coat made it appear larger. In colour it was lighter than that animal, the hair very soft and thick, with an undercoat still finer, like the *pushm* of the goa or gazelle of Thibet.

After "halaling" and taking out the paunch, we hung the body on a tree, to pick up on our way back. We tried a "ruk" of high grass, where, the shikari said, the stags lay in the daytime; but soon found that, unless by the merest fluke in the world, a shot was out of the question, the grass being in many places above my head. It would have been a grand jungle to beat with a line of elephants. We tried forming a line of three, with 50-yard intervals. Just near the end of the ruk, the shikari on my right called out that a stag had got up; and though I ran in the direction he pointed, the stag was too quick for me, and by the time I got outside had disappeared.

The cold at night was intense, and I felt it considerably. My tent was pitched close to a canal, which was frozen hard at the edges, and the floating ice kept up a dull grinding noise, monotonous in the extreme. Nevertheless I was up before daylight, going through the jungle to the open ground, where from a hillock we carefully scanned the country. It was not long before we sighted a herd. My shikari leading the way, we made for a friendly watercourse, deep enough to cover us upright, with a nice even bottom, so that we got on at a great rate, taking an occasional look over the edge to see if they moved. We had got more than half-way, and I was feeling pretty confident, when I heard a sound in the distance which filled me with despair, the human voice divine! It was a beast of a Turki, singing at the top of his voice. The herd were evidently as much annoyed as myself: there they stood, with their heads up, listening to the sound; then turning tail, they trotted into the jungle.

The cause of the disturbance soon appeared, riding a pony. I abused him freely; but as he did not understand my language, it availed nothing. He waved his hand gaily in the direction the deer had taken, and evidently thought he was giving us useful information. I merely said, "Anang is kit," which he seemed to understand, as he moved off rather hurriedly.

Beyond following some more tiger-pugs, I did nothing until the evening, when I arranged a beat for some pheasants. There were not many, but a fine old cock got up with a great fuss and crow, and gave me a grand rocketing shot overhead. He was soon followed by another cock and hen. I found the cock exactly like the English pheasant, without the ring neck, but a slightly pied wing, which did not show much until the bird was in hand. The hen was marked the same as her English sister, but slighter in colour, which gave her a washed-out appearance.

My next game was of another description, and rather turned the tables on me. While looking across the maidan, I became aware of a party of crows making a great fuss, and on asking my shikari what he thought it was, he looked very solemn and said, "Yulwās," the Turki word for tiger. Away I went like a bolt from the blue, and as the grass was only 4 feet high, and less in places, began to hope my chance for a shot was safe.

The crows went on swearing and making a fuss, and as the object that annoyed them was travelling slowly, I soon got within 100 yards. The crows cleared off with a final caw; and cocking my rifle, I hurried on, with a beating heart. Presently out *it* came into full view. *A beast of a dog*, who had been foraging in the night and was making its way back to some shepherd's camp! When it caught sight of me the brute went off as hard as it could, then turned round and began to bark, until I felt much inclined to put up my rifle and stop its noise. These shepherd-dogs are great big hairy animals, very like those seen in Tibet and the Himalayas. They have a good deal more bark than bite in their composition, but the natives have a holy dread of them.

As all the game in the vicinity would be pretty well scared by the noise, I consulted with my shikari, who advised me to move to Shamal, about fourteen miles off. Here I was put up by the headman, who gave me an excellent room and all supplies, and also produced the shikari my late one had mentioned to me as sure to show me sport. Having had a talk with him, I went out and shot a brace of pheasants for the pot.

After dinner, as I was smoking my pipe over the fire, the door opened quietly, and a Chinaman walked in without a word and sat down opposite to me. I was just thinking of hustling him out, when Joker, my dog, who, being black, was not very apparent in the dim light, suddenly awoke: evidently the smell of the Chinaman had stolen on him in his dreams. In a moment he was up, and so was my new friend, who made a spring into the corner of the room, barricading himself with the camp-chair on which he had been sitting. I gave the dog a clout on the head to keep him quiet, and assured my visitor he would not be eaten. He did not, of course, understand my Hindustani, so I shouted for Jaffer and my host, who spoke Chinese, making a sign meanwhile to my friend to smoke a pipe and calm his nerves. He had merely come to pay me a friendly visit, hearing I was a great man travelling about the country. As he was civil enough, and evidently a gentleman in his own country, I gave him a cup of tea, and we had a long talk, during which he told me he had been here on political business, and was now on his way back to Pekin. At Shanghai and Hong-Kong he had seen many foreigners, also English ships, which he greatly admired. On taking his leave, he thanked me for my kind reception.

Going across some gamey-looking country ten miles west of Shamal, we came to the shores of a long lagoon, and pitched our camp on a spot made for the purpose, with nice bare ground for the tents, and plenty dead trees lying about for fuel, the lagoon being handy for water.

I was out before daylight, as the stags go into the long grass when the sun rises, and had not been on the hill long before my shikari said the welcome word "Bōghe," and showed me two stags feeding in a glade about half a mile off. I made a good stalk, and set to work to creep up, pulling off my *charoks*, as they made a crunching noise on the dry grass-stubs, which were crusted over with saltpetre; but even then it was difficult to advance silently, everything being as dry as tinder, and I had to be careful not to break stick or twig. I got a good view of them, and seeing my way to a better shot free from a screen of timber, moved round; but just as I got to the edge, a branch of jow came across my path, and on bending it on one side, it gave with a crack. I heard a snort and a stampede, and was just in time to catch sight of the sterns of the stags disappearing down the glade!

Turning away with my eyes rather on the ground, I heard a rush and a bound in front of me, and caught sight of another stag disappearing behind a clump of trees just ahead. I rushed frantically round, and there, tail on, but looking back, stood the stag, about 50 yards off. There was not a second to be lost, as he stood on the edge of a thick jungle, and nothing for it but a stern shot. I threw up my rifle and fired: he gave a great bound, and disappeared into the wood, whilst I ran round the belt to catch him on the other side. There was a clear view, and he was not in sight, so I pushed my way through the bushes, and there, sure enough, he lay stone dead: my bullet had caught him right in the stern, and penetrated into his vitals.

Seeing him lying there stretched out before me, the usual reaction came on, a feeling of sorrow to have been the death of such a fine beast. But it was too late to moralise, and the practical part had to be seen to, so, shouldering my rifle, I went back to breakfast; after which, getting a couple of ponies, we returned to where the stag lay. I had brought out my tape, so measured him there and then: height 55 inches, girth 57½ inches, elbow to sole of hoof 34 inches, length of back from withers to base of tail 45 inches. The antlers were an even pair of ten points, but not so heavy or so long as those of a good barasingh of Kashmir. The hair I thought a good deal longer and more abundant than the red deer of Europe. The shades were also of a more neutral tint—brown on the back, running into grey down the sides, but darker again on the belly, which was thickly covered with hair.

In the course of my wanderings looking for another shot, I came across a beaten track through the grass, and heard it was made by the Russian expedition under Colonel Peintrow, which we had found encamped near Ak Masjid.

On a grass plain near the river a herd of hinds got up and galloped across me. My shikari was very anxious I should shoot one, but having such a lot of venison in camp, I let them be.

The cold in the mornings now became every

day more intense. I always dreaded coming across a stag in the early hours : my gloves, being made of sheepskin, were not calculated to handle a rifle, and when I pulled them off, my rifle-barrels were so cold that they nearly took the skin off my fingers.

I lost a stag, however, in another way, owing to a stupid habit of the shikaris. With the high grass and scrub jungle, it is always difficult to spot an animal at some distance. Therefore the shikaris, whenever they find a tree they can climb easily, or a hillock rather higher than the rest which will give them a view over the plain, make a point of ascending it. Sometimes these hillocks are crowned with a clump of tamarisk bushes, which makes it all right; but when they are bare at the top, and the man runs up and squats like a crow, the odds are that if there is an animal within a mile, he will see the man before the man sees him.

In spite of having cautioned my shikari about this, the first time I was a little way behind, off he went as usual, and I caught sight of him beckoning to me in the most excited manner. Grasping the situation, and smothering a not very complimentary phrase, I rushed to the top, cocking my rifle as I went, just in time to see a very fair stag galloping away like mad!

Hearing that there were a great many more stags in the jungles beyond Maralbashi, and having had two days without results, I decided to change my ground to that place, where I hoped either to meet or hear from Bower. The wind was intensely cold: I could not ride a yard, but had to walk every inch of the twenty miles to keep myself warm.

The Yangi Hissar at Maralbashi is a fine bastioned fort, well planned and executed, square in shape, and I reckoned each face to be a quarter of a mile. To the south of this lay the old town, consisting of one street with very fair-looking shops and dwelling-houses. I had sent a man on to warn the authorities of my advent, so that I might find some place ready to go to. This is always necessary in a town in Turkistan. In a village it does not signify, as you ride straight in and select the house that pleases you best: the villagers are so civil and hospitable that they are always delighted to put you up. The townspeople are just the reverse, however, and unless some Beg or big man hears of your coming and prepares a place for you, there is nothing for it but to go to the caravanserai, which is generally dirty and cold, and perhaps full of vagrants, so that you have neither peace nor privacy.

On my arrival I was shown into the serai, and a very cold dreary place it was; but on my expressing disapproval of these quarters, they told me there was no other place fit for my reception. These buildings are all of the same type—a large yard surrounded by a high wall with double entrance-gates; a row of stables round the walls, with small feeding-troughs for ponies; a block of mud-brick buildings at the far end, consisting generally of three good-sized rooms opening one into the other; no doors; windows of open lattice-work; and a hole in the roof for the smoke to go out, which in these establishments it always fails to do!

As I intended remaining a day, I made the best I could of the place, hanging up *mundas* in the doorways, blocking the windows, and lighting a blazing fire, which for a wonder burnt all right.

I had a visit from an official of the Amban's, asking the usual questions and wanting to see my passport, which, having given to Bower, I was unable to produce, but explained that my friend, whom I expected to meet, had it, who would no doubt cast up in due time. This was the date we had appointed to meet; but as no word came, I concluded that his business with the Dotai at Kashgar had proved more troublesome than he expected.

I had then a succession of visitors : they were all very nice and civil, with the exception of a party of Chinese soldiers that broke in upon me, and whom I had to eject forcibly.

Thinking it no use waiting, I went on to Charwagh, and when about five miles from this place, came upon the pugs of a large tiger, and the imprints of his hind-quarters where he had evidently sat up, the marks being quite fresh. Every one in Charwagh was in a great state of excitement about it : a man travelling ahead of me had actually seen it sitting there in the middle of the road, and, in a great fright, had made a long *détour* to avoid him.

Beyond the grass jungle in this district was a ridge of stony hills, which ran from the Tian Shan mountains and crossed the Aksu road in a southerly direction. This range, as far as I could see, ran down for some distance towards the Gobi Steppe. The hills were bare, rocky, and very precipitous, resembling the Salt range in the Punjab. In this direction my new shikari said there were lots of maral and some tigers.

We tried it next day, but the grass was so high that without elephants it was utterly hopeless, and I only shot a few pheasants in the evening.

As the only other good beat was un-get-at-able, owing to the river being impossible to ford and the ice not strong enough to bear, I went on to Tumchuk. There I passed through one of the finest jungles I had seen in the country—in some places too thick to shoot in, and almost impenetrable except by crawling.

We moved on to a beautiful tree-jungle quite clear of undergrowth, where, the shikari said, the deer frequently passed in the morning and evening; and their tracks were numerous, but no stags to be seen. Hard by was a cairn of stones, with one or two horns on it, and a pole in the centre from which hung a piece of rag. This *mazar*, he told me, was erected in memory of a man who was pulled off his pony and killed by a tiger some years before. There were a good many in the forest, as I surmised from the number of pugs I had seen, and I always lived in hopes of coming across one; but knowing their habits, and having hunted for them on foot before, I also knew what a fluke it would be.

I searched all the surrounding forests for two days without seeing a horned head, though I came across some hinds, but as I did not require meat, I left them alone. So when a courier came in from Bower telling me not to wait for him, I determined to work on towards Aksu, having heard that beyond that place there was good hunting-ground for stags, jeran, and tigers.

Bower returned my passport, having after some trouble succeeded in getting one for himself, but to do so he had been obliged to take the Dotai into his confidence. He said he had sent off the two men with whom the Commissioner had provided him, also the man whom he had engaged at Yarkand as interpreter, so that he could not start after me until he got another one, which would delay him some days: he therefore begged me not to wait, and he would follow as soon as he could. The news he had received of the murderer was very vague, and he felt his task was almost hopeless.

I went on for twelve miles, walking mostly through jungle, to Jogdŭbŏtak: it all looked likely ground, and there were tracks all about, but I did not meet anything until close to camp, when I kicked up a magnificent boar, which ran across a grass prairie. We rode after him, but having no spears, did not press him hard. There had been sheep grazing all round, so sport here was rather hopeless; and though I followed one stag, I made nothing of it, and continued on my way.

I struck the Aksu road above Chadir Kul, and had another hunt after a stag; but the jungle beat me again, although we came to the very spot where he had lain, and the ground was still warm. We could hear the sticks crack, and something moving ahead, but I strained my eyes in vain for a sight of him; and when we got to the open, the only sign left was his track, which showed that he had gone off at a trot.

My shikari recommended me not to waste more time, but to go on to Shazar, as the snow might come on at any moment, and there was no knowing where the stags might be; for instead of coming to water they would eat the snow, and wander all over the country.

So on Christmas Day I struck my camp, and in a couple of marches reached Chillon, a place of some importance, with a couple of hundred inhabitants. There is a small fort and an Amban, who asked for my passport, but begged to be excused calling in person, as he found it too cold to leave his house. Chinamen feel the cold very much, and never go out in winter if they can avoid it.

From here I went by Bashirak, and sent on notice of my intention of arriving the following day at Aksu. The river was crossed by aid of a temporary bridge, not without some danger and difficulty to my ponies, as it was broken in several places. Below the bridge there were large ferry-boats moored, which are used in summer when the river is too big to be bridged. They were very similar to those used on the Indian rivers, but appeared to be more solidly built. The Yangi-Shahar, or New City, the Chinese fort and quarter, was visible in the distance, and seven miles beyond lay the old city of Aksu.

Four miles from the fort I passed the *karaol* or guard-house, where a few Chinese soldiers were hanging about, but they took no notice of me as I rode by. Skirting round two sides of the fort, I got into a bazaar which extended for half a mile in the direction of Aksu.

L

The country round was a sort of table-land or steppe, which seemed to extend from the lower slopes of the Tian Shan mountains. At the base of the cliff which formed the side of this steppe was the city of Aksu, and between this and that was a tract of cultivated country, rice-fields, and orchards,—a rich alluvial plain, evidently formed by the Aksu river, which no doubt at one time had washed up to this cliff.

The road led along the upper plain, dry and barren, with dust a foot deep for five weary miles, until, coming again to the edge of the cliff, I found the city at my feet. It looked a fine large place, and had once covered an area of four square miles, but was now mostly in ruins, having been destroyed by the Chinese. They had done this, I was told, to clear a site for their own New Town, but then thought better of it, as this part was subject to inundations from the river. A narrow winding road cut out of the cliff, which was here about 300 feet high, took me through the ruins to the city.

The main streets were if anything better built than those of Yarkand, being shaded with matting, and having fine stalls on either side:

boot-shops and coppersmiths were very numerous, and I was told that for boots and copper *chāgōnes* (teapots) Aksu was justly celebrated. In the centre of the city was the Russian serai, where I was received by the Russian Aksakal, and shown into a comfortable room well spread with *mundas* and a good fire blazing on the hearth. This was quite the best serai I had seen in the country, having good rooms with verandahs all round, and a separate yard with stable accommodation. The Aksakal was a very good-looking gentlemanly man, almost European in his manners, well dressed in a dark cloth *choga* lined with fur, a fur cap, and well-made high boots. As soon as we were seated a collation of dried fruit, bread, and tea was brought in.[1] To these I did full justice after my long morning's tramp; and then, lighting my pipe, we settled down for a good talk. He gave me full information as to the sport and shikaris, and kindly took my passport to the *yaman* or palace of the Dotai and Amban, who lived in the Yangi-Shahar.

I then received visits from various merchants

[1] Grapes, melons, apples, &c., are preserved through the winter in a species of silo.

who were also in the serai, and who seemed very good sort of people. A Peshawuri, Mahomed Amin by name, came to visit me, a very good old man, who had been settled there many years. He said he loved the English and their Government, which was the best in the world; therefore was delighted to see me, and was most anxious I should take some money from him, of which, he said, he had plenty. I assured him I was very sensible of the kindness of his offer, but that I had brought all I required with me; besides, as I should probably go back to Europe through Russia, how could I repay him? "Oh," he replied, "you have only to write me a chit, and the signature of the sahib is so good that whenever I return to India, be it years hence, I know I shall get my money back." One of his sons then appeared with a tray of almonds, raisins, &c., which he begged me to accept for my journey. The old man had travelled a great deal, having performed the pilgrimage to Mecca, and had been to Moscow and other parts of Russia, besides going backwards and forwards to India. Now he was trying to arrange his affairs, to go back to Peshawur and end his days in his native place.

Poor old fellow! I heard afterwards he had long been trying to wind up his concerns, and that there was very little hope of his ever accomplishing it.

The New Year began with a heavy fall of snow, and I was glad to be in such good quarters, and determined not to move until the weather cleared.

During the day I had many visitors, amongst them some Russian merchants. These traders have a great advantage over ours, paying less duty and having no difficulty in obtaining passports, which is due to the presence of a Russian consul at Kashgar, who takes care that the Imperial subjects have fair-play; whereas our people have no one to help them—a subject of surprise to the Chinese, who do not understand why we neglect our own interests, they having no objection to a resident British consul in the country, either at Yarkand or Kashgar.

I received the usual supplies from the Dotai and Amban, with a message that when the weather cleared they would call; but as this would involve a visit in return, I begged they would not expose their persons to the inclemency of the weather. The Aksakal brought me next day a very acceptable *nazar*, or gift, from these good people, consisting of some tins of the finest tea, and a very handsome piece of Chinese silk.

By the third day the weather had cleared, and I went off, according to the directions given me, to Karatal by Kumbash. A good deal of snow fell at intervals, and it took two days to get there. I had a letter of introduction from the Aksakal to the Beg, who put me up in good quarters, and promised to send a shikari who knew the country well.

The morning broke clear and fine, the mist and clouds having rolled off, and when I looked out, the most lovely view greeted my eyes of the Tian Shan range, towering aloft full 24,000 feet, the immense height being doubly emphasised by the whiteness of the surrounding country, glistening with freshly fallen snow. The Beg had promised to come early and bring the shikari with him, but he had been sent for in the night by the Dotai, to answer for the life of a man who had been found dead in the snow. However, later in the day, the Yulbeggie of the district appeared, saying he had been sent by the Beg to do my business, and that being something of a shikari himself, he would take me to the best places for game. Accordingly we started for Khotan Kama, where he lived, about twenty miles away. On the way he suggested a hunt for jeran with a trained eagle which he had with him, but we found none. Then he proposed, after our arrival, to have a deer-drive in the forest; but after trotting me about here, there, and everywhere without any result, I came to the conclusion he merely wanted to detain me at his village, so told him I could waste no more time.

After Khotan Kama the country was quite wild, without any signs of cultivation or habitation. The junction of the Aksu and Khotan rivers with the Yarkand river occurs here, and from this point change their names for that of the river Tarim, which runs nearly due east until it empties itself into Lobnor. Near Khotan Kama a ferry crosses the Tarim and connects the road from Khotan to Aksu, which is a good deal used by caravans carrying rice from one town to the other.

For the twenty-four miles of jungle through which we tramped my shikari kept his eagle on his wrist, but it was not until we got to our camping-ground, when he went off by himself to have a last look round, that he had any success, returning with a doe jeran. I was anxious to see the eagle work, and as I could see nothing of a stag, went off with the Yulbeggie in the afternoon to try for another jeran. I was mooning along thinking of something else, when all of a sudden the Yulbeggie started off as hard as he could gallop across the maidan. I followed suit, and soon made out a doe jeran in the distance. It stood and looked at us in amazement, and then cantered off, not very fast, while we still continued our headlong career, every now and then floundering on to our noses over a tussock of grass or into a hole hidden by the snow, until we got to about 100 yards from our game, which only then realised the situation and extended its stride. The shikari now hurled the eagle, which he had unhooked and held clasped to his breast during the run, at the jeran. The eagle, instead of rising like a falcon and sweeping on its prey, flapped along with its great wings quite close to the ground; and although it seemed to fly very slowly, gradually caught up the jeran, which was impeded in its course by the high grass, and at last grabbed it by the rump with its strong talons. It regularly dragged the deer down, and held on for some time, the little gazelle kicking out like mad. We still galloped on, and I wondered what the finish would be. The shikari, when he got up to them, without drawing rein threw himself off his pony and grabbed the deer by the hind-leg, just as it had kicked itself free, and pulling out his knife, cut its throat. It was a most exciting chase, and I enjoyed the gallop immensely. Bob evidently did the same, seeming thoroughly to enter into the sport. On another occasion the eagle, after it was thrown, did not see its quarry, and, after a vague flight, lit on the ground and began to scream; and the next time, when it was more successful, we were too long in coming up, and the deer had shaken it off, going on seemingly none the worse, while the eagle, which was now on the ground, remained there screaming like a fool, without attempting to get on the wing again to follow up its game.

My tent was pitched in a glade by the river, and well sheltered by forest all round; and as there was any amount of fallen trees for fuel, huge fires all about the camp made the place look very comfortable.

The hunt for stags continued unavailing, and I began to think they must be very scarce. My shikari allowed that such was the case, they being so much hunted in the summer, when their horns are in velvet, that being the time they are valued for their medicinal properties.

My next goal was a village called Bashkiok, on the south side of the river, and on the edge of the great Gobi Steppe.

The only sport we had on the road was with two flights of the eagle, after a fox and a hare. The foxes are much like our own in shape and size, but the fur is longer and softer, and rather lighter in colour: they are much prized, and a large trade is done in them. Many are shot by the shikaris, who are very good at imitating the cry of a hare in distress: this never fails to bring up a fox to the gun if within hearing.

The houses at Bashkiok are built in the following rather novel but effective way. The country along the steppe is scattered over with hillocks, formed of dust and soil blown up from the desert. A hillock convenient in size and situation is selected; a square excavation is then dug, which gives a back wall and two side walls; a front wall of mud and wattle is then put up, and the whole roofed over. A fireplace and chimney are dug out of the back wall, and a very comfortable hut is thus made.

The Yubashi or headman came to see me when I had pitched my tent, and brought some grain—a very welcome gift for the ponies. I told him I wanted a shikari, as my present one did not know this country; and he promised to send me the only one there was as soon as he came in from visiting some traps. There was, he said, a large tract of forest full of game, and one tiger that had been a great trouble in the neighbourhood, killing all the sheep, which he begged me if possible to shoot. Of course I readily promised to do so if I got the chance.

Soon after this a cavalcade approached with two bullocks laden with something the nature of which I could not discern, but which, on coming nearer, proved to be portions of a camel, the head just as it had been cut off, and some huge joints of meat. I was much interested, and asked the shikari where he had got it. He said that the camels came to a place on the edge of the great desert, about twenty-five miles off, to drink water and graze on a certain kind of grass that grew there : in his time he had killed several of them there. This seemed an unusual opportunity, and I told him I should like to shoot a specimen. He replied it was very unlikely we should get another, for now that the snow lay about, they went away to the heart of the desert, and did not return to drink at the pools until it had all disappeared, as the snow sufficed for their wants. However, we might try, and failing my getting one, I could take this head and skin.

I tried some camel-steak for dinner, but found it very tough.

The specimen the shikari had brought back was a full-grown female, and, judging by her teeth, pretty old. She must have been a very handsome beast, and in size much the same as the tame species. The head was beautifully shaped, and showed high breeding—very broad across the forehead, with a tapering muzzle. In colour the hair was a bluish grey, rather short, but close and fine, with an undergrowth of *pushm;* on the head it was so fine as to be more like fur. The humps, of which there were two,-were small, and the animal altogether quite a different species from the ordinary Bactrian camel used in the country, and bred in the hills.

The shikari was a very intelligent, well-informed man, and gave me much information on our way to the desert. Amongst other things, he pointed out a long-shaped sandhill on which there was a graveyard, the origin of which no one knew. I went up to look at it, and found the wind had drifted the sand away, and the graves were open: the skeletons were in a very perfect condition, owing to the dryness of the atmosphere, and lay in various directions, the heads and feet pointing all ways, which showed they were not Mohammedans. There were no relics to be found in the sand, except some bits of rough broken pottery, which were too defaced and fragmentary to convey any information as to the period in which they were made.

The pools in this part were so brackish as to be quite undrinkable, only camels and jeran being able to use the water. The region, consequently, was perfectly barren, even of nomad shepherds. Collecting some snow to melt off the ice of one of these pools, I found it so briny as to be unfit to drink—indeed what we took from off the sand was slightly impregnated with salt from the soil.

When we got as far as the part known as Takla Makhan, the tradition concerning which I knew vaguely, we sat down on a sandhill while my shikari related the following legend.

CHAPTER IX.

EXPEDITION TO KALMUK.

THE LEGEND OF TAKLA MAKHAN—AN UNEXPECTED SHOT—ARRIVAL OF BOWER—COMFORTABLE QUARTERS—A VILLAGE DANCE — WITH THE KALMUKS — THE TUNKTCHI MAKES DIFFICULTIES — ABOVE THE REGION OF WOOD—FROZEN OUT—THE KHAN'S MOTHER—RETURN TO SHAH YAR—A WILD SWAN—A DEER-DRIVE—BACK AT AKSU—CHINESE COURT OF JUSTICE—SUMMARY PUNISHMENT—GIVING A LESSON—A FRIENDLY ESCORT—THE CHUNKOO'S ‘BAND—FRESH HUNTING-GROUNDS—*OVIS CAROLINI*—ACROSS THE STEPPES—IMPERIAL GROUSE—KASHGAR.

"ONCE upon a time, it might be four or five centuries ago, a kingdom which was called Takla Makhan existed. It extended from Khotan on the south-west, in a long strip of country watered by the Khotan, Yarkand, and Tarim rivers, as far as Pop Mor, or maybe beyond. It was said to be thickly populated and well watered, containing about four hundred and fifty towns and villages.

"At the time of its destruction it was governed by two kings named Tŭkterĭchĭt and Nŭkterĭchĭb, who were said to be excellent rulers, and much beloved by the people. They did not appear to live at any one place, but travelled about looking after the country, very much as a district officer in India does at the present day. Owing to this, everything in the country was very prosperous, and the people contented and happy.

"These kings were supposed to be of Mongol origin, and had quantities of camels and horses. For some reason, however, God was displeased with the people, probably because they were Buddhists, and so He commanded a mighty south wind to blow, and after it commenced the sky grew black, and an immense wall of sand came up with the wind. Soon the country was enveloped in pitchy darkness, so dark that no one could see; the sand became thicker and thicker, so that no one could breathe, until at last none remained alive in the whole land. All the fertile tracks up to the great rivers were smothered with sand, so that now only the narrow strip of forest jungle which extends between the desert and river remains."

This story was told in Turki, and interpreted

by old Rahamut, my groom, whom I always took about with me as interpreter, and it at once confirmed my belief in the tame origin of the present so-called wild camels and horses found in these regions. The horses, I had been told by those who had seen them,—amongst others old Rahamut and Barat Akhone, a previous shikari,—inhabit the edges of the desert. They go in herds, vary as much in colour as the tame ones, and have long hair and flowing manes and tails. In height they are pretty much the same as the ponies of the country, 13.3 or thereabouts. They are very wild, are sometimes shot, but never caught.

The camels also vary in colour, like tame ones, from ashy white, running into the sort of blue brown of the specimen that I had, to nearly black. These variations in colour are a great point against their indigenous origin. They do not show any of the characteristics of the Bactrian camel, now in general use, and must belong to another breed, probably brought from China.

After discussing Takla Makhan and the wild camels, my shikari said he would take me to the place where he had killed the last one. It was accompanied by two half-grown young ones, which he had followed for some time, as they seemed inclined to remain in the neighbourhood —probably looking for their mother, poor beasts! —but they were careful not to let him get within shot. He showed me their tracks all about, and, soon after, the spot where he had murdered the mother, the marks in the sand and the blood showing quite fresh. I should very much like to have seen—but did not feel at all inclined to shoot—one, after all I had heard.

On the way home we met the ponies going off somewhere in a gang: they were evidently disgusted with the saltness of the water, and were going in search of something sweeter. We drove them back to camp, and finding one or two guilty of being the ringleaders of this insubordination, tied them up for the night.

There being no prospect of a sight of a camel while this snow lay about, I returned by Bashkiok towards Shah Yar, hoping for some news of Bower.

Going out one morning very early, I was following the tracks of a herd of deer, when, to my astonishment, a pair of antlers suddenly appeared over a clump of bushes, and a stag in all its glory walked out into the open and stood broadside to me, little knowing how it was tempting Providence, to say nothing of myself. I was in a very comfortable position, within 100 yards, so drew a bead and let him have it. The hinds started in every direction at the report, but he never moved. I felt sure I had not missed, but gave him the left barrel, when he quietly sank to the ground.

When I went up and turned him over, I found both bullets within an inch of each other, just in the right place, and on taking out the "gralloch," found they had penetrated the heart. This was another of those instances with which one sometimes meets, when a bullet through the heart does not produce instantaneous death in an animal. He was a big stag, and carried ten points, but his antlers were not at all good.

In the evening, when about half a mile from camp, and it was getting rather dark, we suddenly stopped, hearing something moving in the jungle. From the sound, they were big animals, and coming slowly our way. It was getting darker and darker every minute. At last the sound seemed to approach the end of the glade on which we stood, and I got my rifle ready. Out stepped the leading beast of the herd, one of my own rascally ponies! Presently the whole gang emerged. It was more than lucky I did not shoot one, for had it been a very little darker I should most likely have done so.

The shepherds having come into the forest, we struck camp, and finding the district for nearly twenty miles was overrun, went on to the village of Sierak, and from there to Shah Yar. Here I was met by a sort of orderly officer of the Beg's, and conducted to a capital house just outside the bazaar, where I soon had a mass of visitors, and amongst others a man who had just come in from the direction of Kuchar, and gave me the welcome news that he had passed Bower on his way. This was capital; so I settled myself comfortably, and set to work skinning the camel's head : it was frozen so hard that I had to thaw it before the fire. The body skin I had been trying to dry in the sun; but even at mid-day it had very little power over the cold air, and I had not as yet succeeded.

About five o'clock Bower arrived. He had sent men out in all directions — after Dad Mahomed — whom he expected to be back in about a month, when he should have to return to receive them. I had hoped we might have gone on together and explored the eastern Tian Shan; but it would have taken too long, so we enjoyed a couple of days of each other's company, and then I went on towards Kalmuk, while Bower started to hunt stags in the jungle beyond Shah Yar.

On my way I broke my journey at Charcken and Kuchar. At the latter, unfortunately, it was market-day, the place crowded, and all the serais full and dirty, until at last I came to the Andigami serai—*i.e.*, one frequented by Russian Turkistan traders from that place. The Malik immediately showed me to an excellent apartment, which he had built as a house of prayer, and also to place at the disposal of any distinguished visitors. He treated me right royally, giving me the best he had, and begged to be allowed to cook a meal for me. Also, as he spoke Chinese, he offered to take my passport to the Amban the following day; for as it was a big day with the Chinese, he would be drunk, and incapable of transacting business. I was quite ready to stay in such good quarters for one day. And the following, fortunately for me, was a case of "the same drunk as yesterday" with the great man; so visits and presents, of which of a suitable kind I was running short, were dispensed with.

Leaving the suburb, I saw a long stretch of water, and learnt there was a lake fed by the stream we had crossed, extending about eight miles east and west, and was as salt as the sea. It was a long weary tramp to Yakka, where I found a crowd assembled on a sort of village green, forming a circle round the lads and lasses, who were disporting themselves in some kind of country dance. I joined the throng as a spectator, but soon found myself surrounded instead, and the dancing ceased. Being anxious to see the performance, I asked them to continue, which after a while they did. It seemed to be a dance very similar to that of the Bhots or Sadakis,—a slow measure, with the same sort of hand gesture, to the accompaniment of a small drum and rude sort of wooden instrument.

The country through which I was travelling was uninteresting, and the marches, daily from twenty to thirty miles, very wearisome, being mostly over a stony sort of moraine that comes down from the mountains, and so cold that I walked the greater part of the way. Passing Awat and Bugar, the latter a place of some importance, having a Chinese fort and Amban, I caught up a party of native travellers, among whom was a pilgrim—or Hadji, as they are called—from Mecca. He had come by way of India, which, he said, in spite of the hardships encountered (for it was in the month of December) on crossing the big passes,—Karakoram, Kilian, &c.,—was infinitely better than by Russian Turkistan and Constantinople, and much cheaper; but out of his seven companions, one after another had been taken ill between Karakoram and the Kilian, and had died from the effects of the cold!

At Yangi-Shahar I found the people all agog about two tigers. It appeared they always marauded together, and divided their favours between this and Chadir, a stage about eighteen miles farther on. A deputation came praying me to slay these animals. From what I had heard, the tigers never returned to a kill, and ranged all over a large area of country, chiefly high grass and jungle; therefore to hunt for them would be almost useless. Having explained this to them, I promised to do my best if I saw my way to a shot; but as no one knew their exact whereabouts, I considered it pretty hopeless. The last news of them was from Chadir, where some sheep had been killed three days previously.

On my arrival there, the news soon spread that I had come to kill the redoubtable tigers, and the Beg shortly appeared. I told him, unless I got authentic *khubber* as to the tigers' whereabouts, there was no use thinking of it. He promised to do his best to get information, and if they were anywhere in the neighbourhood, would turn out the whole place to beat up Mr and Mrs Stripes. His ideas on the subject of beating were rather crude; and when I pointed out to him that, if he followed the plan he proposed, any of the beaters might get killed, he said that would not the least signify as long as we got the tigers! However, no news of them coming, I told the Beg that if he could do better on my return, I would see what could be done.

I had a long march to Charcken, and it was dark before I got near; so, seeing some men who looked like Chinese hanging about, I called out "Chin, Chin." They came running up, and one of them speaking Turki, I found they were Kalmuks. They showed me the best house in the village, the very one out of which they came, where a blazing fire was excessively welcome. My escort followed me in, so I begged them to be seated, and set to work to find out all about their spokesman and his comrades, who were the first of the Kalmuki race I had met. They had taken service as soldiers under the Chinese, like many of their countrymen, and when they heard I was going to visit their country, related wonderful tales of the sport to be obtained in the mountains. They seemed so chummy and jolly, more like Goorkas than any of the other natives I had met, that I took quite a fancy to them.

As the next morning snow came on hard and fast after our start, and with it such an intensely bitter wind, and there being no possible stopping-place for thirty-one miles, I gave orders to return, and was quite glad to be back, with my Kalmuki friends about me.

When the storm was past I pushed on to Kurla, where a Turki, sent by the Aksakal of Kurla, met me and saw to my wants.

Kurla was formerly a place of importance, and strongly fortified, the walls being six miles round, now mostly in ruins as well as the houses within. However, I was very comfortably located, and found a stove in my room, which looked quite civilised. I had to halt for a day or two, to collect fresh supplies and fit out for an expedition into Kalmuk and up into the Tian Shan mountains, where, report said, great sport was to be obtained — *Ovis poli*, stags, bears, leopards, &c.

The Kalmuki recommended by the Aksakal came to see me. He was a fine big man, and, excepting his pig-tail, might have been an Englishman; but he was not encouraging. According to him, Yulduz was a fine sporting-place, but not at this season: the cold was so great, and the snow so deep, that no one could live there. He described it as a high open valley in the heart of the Tian Shan range, approached by roads from Kuldja and Kalmuk, both over high passes. According to my map, the Kashgar river has its source there. Running through Kalmuk, it falls into a lake at Karachar, and emerging again, flows in a south-westerly direction to Kurla, where I found it, after which its course is not properly defined; but, from information given me, it must sweep round, until it runs again towards Lobnor and joins the Tarim, before it empties itself into that lake.

The passes into Yulduz were the difficulty, and there was no road up the Kaidugol river. From

Kalmuk to Umrutsi, the Kalmuki said, there was a good enough road for ponies over one or two passes which were open all the year round, which would lead me to good Ovis-ground, but that there was absolutely no fuel of any sort—neither wood, *burtsa*, nor even yak's dung. This was rather a bad look-out; for though the cold where I had been travelling was severe enough, 15° to 20° below zero, I had always been able to get plenty of wood for fires when in camp, and did not mind; but this, intensified by higher regions and wind, which, at night especially, is bad in the mountains, would be far from pleasant. In spite, however, of his advice, having made up my mind to try it, I told him I should start, and if my position in the mountains was untenable, I could but return.

Hearing that the Beg and an envoy sent by the Dotai of Karachar were coming to see me, I had to arrange my room for a function, and improvise seats—for, since the Chinese rule, the Turkis with any pretensions to rank think it *infra dig.* to sit on their heels, as their forefathers did before them. Although the Beg was a Mussulman, he was got up in Chinese clothes, a mandarin hat, and pig-tail all complete. The tail was but a poor little grey thing, about 4 inches long! The envoy was better looking than most Chinamen, and also was dressed in his Sunday's best. They were accompanied by another Chinese official, and all the Aksakals and head merchants of the place, quite a crowd. The envoy, who was a colonel in the Chinese army, brought me an invitation from the Dotai to visit Karashar; but I excused myself, returning my thanks to his highness, and trusting to have that honour later, but that now I was anxious to push on to my hunting-grounds. The usual passport business was gone through, and after an hour's talk my visitors departed, and having secured a guide, I prepared for an early start.

Following the river for some distance, we entered a narrow gorge cut by the stream through a rocky spur of the Tian Shan range, which after about four miles brought us to a *karaol* or custom-house at the head of the defile, and then emerged on to the plain through which the river flows from Kashgar: then, turning north-north-west, we crossed some ridges of low hills overlooking a flat plain, surrounded on two sides by high mountain-ranges, which the guide said was the Kalmuk country. We travelled on until about half-way to that capital, when we made a halt in a tract of low thin forest, where there was grass and water, but not a dry stick to be found : while hunting about for some, I came upon a Kalmuki camp, and as they offered to supply me with wood, and as there was a well handy, I made my camp near them. They helped me to pitch the tents, and brought milk as well as wood and water.

These people were very pleasing, so good-tempered and jolly—quite a contrast to the lazy curious Chinese or the apathetic Turki. They live in *yurts* like those of the Kirghiz, and were altogether nomads ; for until the Chinese built a palace for the Khan, there was not such a thing as a house in the country. They do not cultivate at all, living on the produce of their flocks. Their habits, unfortunately, are dirty, and they are very fond of the filthy drink with which the Chinese supply them, and incessantly smoke a strong green tobacco. Their religion is Lama Buddhism ; and they neither bury nor cremate their dead, simply lay out the corpse, which it is the duty of the dogs to eat, outside their camp. It does so happen that sometimes even the dogs refuse this gruesome meal, which they say is a sign that the man must have lived a very bad life indeed.

The cold at night was intense, a piercing wind sweeping down from the mountains.

The capital of Kalmuk consists in the *yaman* of the Khan, and a small serai built after the Chinese pattern; in this the Khan administers justice. Round these buildings were pitched, without regard to order or form, about two hundred *yurts*.

On arriving I sent for the Khan's Tunktchi, or secretary, who seemed very much astonished to see me, wondering, no doubt, what sort of an animal I was; and he evidently did not believe a word on being told I was travelling for sport, and that I had a passport which I should ask him to take to the Khan with my respects as soon as my things came in, and beg him to give me a room in the serai. He said he would go and see the Khan about it, and meantime I had better sit in his *yurt*. On his return he brought permission to put up in the serai, but said I could neither go to the Khan nor could the Khan come to me, as he was observing a religious retreat and not allowed to see any one, mentioning he was a very religious man, and had only just returned from a pilgrimage to Zassah. I was by no means disappointed being saved these formal visits, though I naturally conveyed a different impression to the Tunktchi.

I applied for a guide, but they were evidently suspicious as to my intentions, and always made excuses, saying one had not turned up. At last he brought a man, whom I soon found out through an interpreter was no good, and told the Tunktchi so, and that I must have a proper man. I had come a long way, I said, to get some shooting, and if my journey was to no purpose his face would be blackened. This had the desired effect, in so far that he suggested my taking the Kalmuki I had met at Kurla, which suited very well, as he spoke Turki, and I could converse with him through Jaffer.

Terms were quickly settled, only the Kalmuki said quietly that he must ask me to pay in advance, as the Tunktchi required a *dusturi*—a commission of about half what I paid; but he promised to take me quickly on to ground where I should have as much sport as I wanted in a week. I handed over a hundred tongas— about twenty rupees—quite delighted to settle the business. But in the evening Jaffer came to say that for some reason the man would not be allowed to go with me, for the Khan was very angry with him, and had sent him back to his village. Furious at this, I sent for the Tunktchi. That worthy did not appear until quite late, and told the same story, but said he would bring another guide the following morning.

At daylight I was up and gave the order to load the ponies, which brought the Tunktchi on the scene. I told him I was going to start at once for the mountains, and if the Khan did not provide me with a guide, I should probably lose my way, when there was no knowing what might happen; and if the matter came to the ears of the Chinese they would punish the Khan, for they considered me as their guest whilst travelling in the country: also, that I knew the man I paid the day before was in Kalmuk, and that he lied when he said he had been sent away. The ponies being ready, I gave the word to march, which brought my friend to his senses, and he hastily despatched a messenger, who in ten minutes was back, bringing the guide with him, who, as I felt sure, had been handy all the time.

We took a northerly direction across the Kalmuki plain, over several stony moraines, until we came to the mouth of a deep gorge through which a fair-sized river ran. There was a pretty good pony-road running through it, which led to Umrutsi. Our guide said he constantly went trading expeditions by it to that place from Karachar, where he lived. There were three passes to cross, none difficult, although one was pretty high, and the road was open all the way, the only hardship being the total absence of fuel after the first three stages, there being about ten in all.

It was a very fine gorge, with great barren cliffs of dark granite rising on each side, and at the bottom along the river, grass and jungle, in which grew poplar, aspen, and willow. But the wind blew down it cold and bleak from the snows above; so that when, towards evening, we got to a snug-looking camping-ground under a high cliff, and a fine lot of dead wood in the river-bed, we were glad to rest over a blazing fire, while the ponies were well provided with grass.

Two nullahs joined the valley farther up, after which the country opened out, with grass-prairies and variegated belts of timber. On these prairies at intervals were Kalmuki camps, with flocks of sheep, cattle, and goats.

I had expected to see yak again in these hills, but was told none were to be found in the Tian Shan. There were, however, ponies of a sturdy breed that have the reputation of doing better work than any others in Central Asia, but they are very bad-tempered, and very difficult to manage about feeding at first, as they will not touch grain of any sort, and eat nothing but green food or hay. They stand on an average from 13 to 13.3 hands in height. The ponies from the "Cossack" country, as the district beyond the Tian Shan range towards Illi is called, are very similar, with the exception that they run a little bigger and are better tempered.

Our camp that night was the last where we might expect timber, the guide said, as the following day we should get above the region of wood, and should have difficulty even in finding sufficient for cooking purposes, which was rather sad hearing.

As we advanced up the river the jungle in the river-bed gradually decreased, and we passed the last Kalmuki camp, beyond which was no fuel, and the cold was so intense that no one remained in the winter. The hills on either side were less precipitous than lower down, and covered with the same species of fine grass which is found on the lower pamirs, and is highly prized for grazing.

In passing a Kalmuki camp, one of the men came to see who I was, and when he heard what I had come for, told me that a few days previously some arkars, or female Ovis, were in the hills above, and offered to show me the ground; but on telling him that I only wanted gooljas, he said I should have to go a long way, where the ground was covered with snow, and where the cold was so intense we could not possibly exist, owing to the total absence of fuel. As the sun was shining, and there was not much wind, I rather laughed at the idea; but when the sun went down shortly after, and a strong wind came down the valley, I began to realise the situation. Though the camp was placed in the most sheltered spot to be found, bad was the best; and though we had brought a small supply of wood for cooking purposes, my cook complained he could neither get the water to boil nor the food to cook. At last I got some sort of a meal; but the cold was now so intense I could not sit up to smoke a pipe, therefore turned in with all my clothes on, and all the rugs and sheepskins over me. I pulled the rugs over my head, but it was no good,—my feet were stone cold, and my breath froze on the blankets: it was certainly the most uncomfortable night I ever spent. If I felt it, how much more must my followers and ponies have done so!

It was a disappointment to give up the hunt for the "Carolini" sheep, but madness to continue under such circumstances. I therefore decided to return, to the great relief of my men, whom I found, soon after daybreak, huddled together in their tent. They managed to light a fire in it, and made some tea, which revived us a little. We then went to see after the ponies. Anything more miserable I never saw in my life: they looked as if they were cut out of wood. Going up to the one given me by Mahomed Unis, and giving him a push to wake him up, he just tumbled over on his side, and we had great difficulty in getting him up again. They were too cold to eat, and there was nothing for it but to wait until the sun rose to thaw them. Poor old Rahamut, my pony-man, had his ears frost-bitten, but by dint of bathing them with cold water we got them right.

When we got off at last, we were a very cripply

lot—the poor ponies scarcely able to move; but they warmed up gradually as we got lower down, and the sun made itself felt. Had I continued, it would have been a difficult matter to have kept them alive: the old stagers would eat snow in default of water, but the others did not understand it. What a treat a fire was that night, to be sure, after being half perished with cold, and not much food to help one to resist it!

We retraced our steps much in the same direction as that by which we had come, making for the places where dead wood was lying in abundance, and using it with no sparing hand. When within five miles of Kalmuk I met the mother of the Khan, who was going into camp for a change, and was very pleased to have the chance of making her acquaintance, having heard much about her. During the minority and absence of her son in Shaza, she had governed the country; and so well had she fulfilled the task, that the people were very sorry when the Khan returned. She was an active woman of about fifty years of age, good-looking, and with plenty of character in her expression, quite European in type, and not a trace of the Mongol about her excepting in her dress, which consisted of a loose *choga* dressing-gown of dark cloth lined with fur, voluminous pyjamas thrust into a pair of riding-boots with high heels, and on her head a round cap of brown cloth turned up with fur. She rode a fine Kalmuki pony at the head of her retainers, and when she met me, asked why I had returned so soon? I must confess to feeling rather small, having to acknowledge to being driven back by the cold: she, however, thought it a rash experiment going into these mountains in the depth of winter, and did not seem surprised at my non-appreciation of the climate.

On arriving, I informed the Tunktchi I would now pay the Khan a visit if he would receive me, but he said that unfortunately his religious duties would not admit of it for a few days; so I had to forego the pleasure, which did not amount to much, certainly, except a slight curiosity to see the inside of the *yaman.*

From what I could ascertain, this State has a poor revenue, and is under the protection of, and kept up by, the bounty of the Chinese Government, who pay over a sum equal to £2000 of our money yearly, in exchange for which a hundred or so Kalmuki men are supplied to the Chinese Government in Turkistan as soldiers.

There being no inducement to remain here longer, I decided to return to Shah Yar by the way I came, and try and catch Bower, if he had not already returned to Kashgar. However, on getting to Shah Yar I found he had left three days previously. After an unsuccessful trip for stags in the direction of Lobnor, I determined to follow, thinking I should find him camped somewhere on my old ground across the river; but on making inquiry, I heard that the ice on the river had begun to break up, and that Bower had just got over by the skin of his teeth. So there was nothing for it but to travel back on the left bank, and look for stags in the jungles on this side.

Having secured a guide, we started on the 14th of March. It was always the same sandy sort of desert country, covered at intervals with open tamarisk jungle. There were frequent tracks of jeran antelope, but no traces of maral.

Crossing a water-channel, a tributary of the Tarim river, we camped in a belt of timber, and here I found a collection of the curious dug-out dwellings of the country. Near them was a camp of inhabitants, who were shepherds, and who brought me little offerings of their flocks—milk, &c.—in return for which they were made quite happy by some odds and ends out of my pack of piece-goods. Starting well ahead of the ponies, and rifle in hand, we went in the direction where a shepherd reported having seen a herd of deer with two stags in it. There was very little high timber about, but a great deal of dense high grass in patches, interspersed with hillocks covered with *jow* or tamarisk. The ground lay low, and was evidently under the influence of floods from the Tarim river, for here and there were lagoons and water-channels; but as these were frozen over, they did not impede our progress much.

In places there were patches of open water, ducks and geese were very thick, and every now and then a skein of the latter would fly overhead. Approaching one of these lagoons, with rather more open water than the others, I saw that it was alive with wild-fowl, so determined to crawl up and see what manner of birds they were. I had left my gun for convenience' sake, and they of course allowed me to get quite close to them; and while looking them carefully over, noting that they consisted of all the species well known in Europe in the way of ducks and grey geese, out from behind a tuft of grass sailed a lovely swan.

He looked every inch a king as he swam along, the crowd of lesser fowl making way for him. So far as I could see, he appeared to be identical with our tame species. Crawling carefully back, I left the place without disturbing the birds, intending to return in the morning for a shot at the swan; but when I got there the lagoon was frozen hard and not a thing in it, except a small flock of geese sitting on the ice. So hard had it frozen during the night, that the ice on the shallow end bore my weight without breaking.

Wending my way along the jungle of tamarisks and round the hillocks, all of a sudden I heard a snort and a rush in front, and just got a glimpse of a stag as he disappeared. The whole thing was done so quickly, that even had I been at full-cock with the rifle at the ready, I should hardly have had time for a snap-shot. From the passing glimpse of his dun carcase he must have been a full-grown beast.

When we had gone about sixteen miles from the last camp, we came to a great open grass-prairie, extending for some miles in a westerly direction. To the east was forest, hillocks, and high grass, where the shikari said there was always a chance of a stag. From one of these hillocks we made out a herd of deer on the move, and followed them to some high grass, where they stopped to feed. To my disappointment they were all hinds, so I let them be, much to the disgust of the shikari, who was, as is usual with his kind, anxious for meat. There being no signs of a stag, but a good many tracks of jeran about, I told him to keep a sharp look-out, and if I saw a buck jeran I would shoot him. By-and-by we saw some red objects moving through the grass, which we could tell were jeran, and when they got on to the more open ground, I made out their horns with the glass. Bidding the shikari stay where he was and see where they went in case I lost sight of them, I marked well the direction, and proceeded to stalk, and very soon got to my point: there, about 150 yards off, was a buck jeran. He stood grazing broadside on to me on a hillock, which raised him above the grass. The bullet sped true, and over went the little animal dead on the grass. Up came the shikari in great glee, knife in hand, all ready to turn him into lawful food. Telling him to cut his throat and carry him into camp,

I took another turn through the jungle, but only saw a few doe jeran and the slot of a stag, which, though I hunted early and late, never showed a sign of his horn. So we moved on to a fresh bit of forest, keeping along the banks of the river for some ten miles, after which we had to cross it.

The ice was rotten, and though it would bear a man, was not good enough for a pony. The channel being only about 4 feet deep, we determined to break up the ice as best we could and make the ponies ford. Taking off the loads, these were soon carried across; then we set to work with the first pony. Tying a long halter to each side of his head-stall, with a man on each side, he was led on to the ice, which gave with him at once: he then tried to scramble and flounder on again, and broke another junk. In this way he was got over, and a channel cut, which the others waded through without difficulty.

Skirting a big marsh which was swarming with ducks and geese, at which I did not shoot, not wishing to make a noise, I came to a fairly open tract. Along the banks and on the sandy soil were tracks of a big stag. While hunting about I got separated for a short time from the shikari, and when he rejoined me, he said that soon after I got out of sight a big stag rose up from the grass where he had been lying and ran past within 50 yards of him. Was there ever such luck!

In the afternoon a dust-storm began to blow, and all the ponies strayed, so Mahomed Atta went after them. Shortly after they came in of their own accord: Mahomed Atta was not with them, and as it was dark we feared he had lost his way. All about the camp there were hillocks covered with high reeds: these we set a light to, at intervals, up to ten o'clock; but as he did not turn up, we concluded he had stayed with some shepherds for the night. We waited a while before striking camp, leaving a man behind to show him the way we had taken. Soon after we had pitched the tents on the banks of the Tarim river, he came in. He said he got benighted and lost his way in the dusk, and after wandering about for some time, gave it up, and, lighting a fire, went to sleep until the morning, when he found his way back and followed us.

Getting back to my old camp between Koronikul and Bugus Kungurga, I found a good many shepherds about, and determined to try a deer-drive, which my shikari agreed was the only way to get a shot in these dense jungles; but he only succeeded in getting four men, which with three of my own made seven. The great difficulty was to get a possible place to drive, for the forest was very extensive and thick; the beaters also found it very hard to keep in line, as they could not take a point to move upon, and kept losing sight of one another. At the end of every beat (and I tried it for three days) one of them had always put up something, but nothing ever came within sight of where I was posted,—the deer evidently would not drive.

It was now the 27th of March, and the stags, it struck me, were losing their horns, so I determined to waste no more time, but return to Aksu, and go from there to Usturfan, as it would probably now be warmer in the mountains; and I was very keen to get one of the Tian Shan sheep, which by all accounts were plentiful in the hills above that place. Accordingly I made straight tracks by Bugus Kungurga, Khotan Kama, and Karatal, for Aksu, which we reached in eight days.

The Russian Aksakal met me outside the town,

and took me to his house, begging me to put up there during my stay. I told him I should prefer, with his permission, to live in some place outside the town; so, after drinking tea, we proceeded to hunt for a villa residence in the suburbs, and found a convenient place, an orchard with a sort of little bungalow in it, surrounded by a good high wall, which I thought would protect me from the prying eyes of the public, as it was my intention to remain a few days to refit and feed up the ponies, who were getting rather low in flesh from constant work.

Going one day to visit the Amban and Dotai, I found a great crowd in the courtyard of the *yaman*, and was told the Amban was administering justice, and settling a case about a Beg in the neighbourhood. The crowd was composed of all the inhabitants of his district, some for and some against him. His enemies accused him of undue oppression, in fact robbery, while his friends said it was all humbug! On inquiring how the Amban was settling the case, they said that the matter was being put to the vote—those in the Beg's favour in one court, those against him in another: if the majority were on the side of the Beg, those against him would get a sound thrashing! After a little while the crowd was separated, and penned up like a flock of sheep : those who accused the Beg, being in the minority, were now going to catch it! Eight or ten soldiers next appeared on the scene, armed with sticks, and walked in among the wretched people, thrashing them in the most unmerciful way. Having settled this little matter, the Amban sent word he was ready to receive me, so I proceeded to the hall of audience, when the large doors were thrown open, and the great man met and led me in. We exchanged the usual civilities, drank tea, and smoked a pipe together, and then taking my leave, I went on to the Dotai. On asking for him at his *yaman*, I was told he was not able to receive company, some friends having come to pay him a visit—they were all dead drunk together!—so left my card and rode back to Aksu.

Just outside the city there was a fortified barrack in which were quartered a lot of Chinese soldiers, who gave me a proof that the old Chinese saying, " We do not make nails out of good iron, or soldiers out of good men," is founded on fact. As a rule, when I passed by any of these soldiers they made what I gathered to be impertinent and insolent remarks; but not understanding the language, I was a little shy of jumping on them in case of being mistaken.

This afternoon, on my way home from these visits, half a dozen Celestials were working in a field close to the road. As usual, they began shouting, so I rode up a little nearer, when one of them suddenly strode up and spat in my pony's face. This was a clear case and no mistake; so, kicking my pony in the ribs, I was on him in a couple of bounds, taking him rather by surprise, and with my heavy riding-whip gave him one or two real good ones across the face. I was so much engaged with him that I did not notice at the first moment that his comrades had come to his rescue, and were hammering me on the back with their gardening tools; but as my pony was a pretty big one, and they were none of them very full-sized specimens of humanity, they could not reach my head, or do me much damage.

The man whom I had struck took up a stone and threw it at me, but it fortunately missed, and I succeeded in giving him another good one across the face. There then came a short pause in the proceedings, and one of them—rather a better-looking man than the rest — began talking in Turki. My orderly, a servant of the Aksakal, who was with me, and who had kept at a discreet distance during the fray, now came up, and told them, as far as I could understand, that I was a friend of the Amban, &c.

Considering I had sufficiently punished the chief offender, I turned away and rode home. Soon after, the Aksakal came to my bungalow in a great state of mind, saying he must report the matter to the Chinese authorities. I told him not to do so, as I had punished "John" sufficiently. But he said the Amban would certainly hear about it, and if he did not take personal notice, would call him over the coals, as he was in a manner responsible for my safety in the place. I therefore told him just to explain the matter, and say that the soldiers had been impertinent, and that I felt called upon to punish the chief offender with my own hand, and was quite satisfied. I had, in fact, marked my man on the face for some time to come, quite sufficiently to serve as a moral lesson for him and his friends in the future to leave harmless Britishers alone.

The wall round the orchard where my tent was pitched was about 8 feet high, and as I sat smoking under an apple-tree next morning I heard the discordant voices of the Chinamen on the other side. Presently there was a scramble, and a yellow moonlike face appeared over the top. The moment he caught sight of me he dropped. A consultation followed, and they moved round to the gateway. Not being quite sure as to what this might portend, I armed myself with a big stick which I kept handy for such a purpose, and took up my position at the door of the house. My visitors stopped at the gate; so calling to Jaffer, I told him to go and find out what they wanted. As the talking continued for some time, I strolled up to the gate. They were my friends of the previous day, and the one who spoke Turki said they came to ask why I had attacked them. I replied I had done so because one of them had insulted me, and that for the future they had better remember that if they insulted an Englishman they would certainly meet the same reward. The spokesman then said, had they been aware I was a great man they would not have done so, but they thought I was a Russian, to which people they have a great dislike; so telling them to be more careful another time, we separated amicably.

Having completed my preparations for my projected trip to Usturfan and the mountains beyond, I was escorted part of the way by the Aksakal and his followers. Mahomed Amin, the old Peshawuri merchant, who had been so civil to me on my previous visit to Aksu, turned up just as we were starting, saying he intended to see me as far as Usturfan. Expressing my gratitude for his kind intentions, I begged him to remember he was an old man, and that I did not want him to risk the fatigue of two long marches at that season; for although when the sun was out it was fairly warm, the nights were still very cold. But nothing would induce him to give up the plan. He said I was the only Englishman he had met for a long time, and he had such a love and respect for our Government in India, that the least he could do was to show me attention.

Our road took us up the left bank of the Aksu river, when we turned westward and crossed the river, which was here broken up into channels on a wide bed. As the snow on the mountains had not yet begun to melt, the fords were quite shallow, and all the ponies got over without much difficulty. Selecting the best house we could find in a village called Barmi, we spent the first night there.

The next place we came to was Achtagh, at the extremity of a range of rocky hills which come down from the west and enclose the valley in which Ushturfan is situated on the south. To the north we saw the great Tian Shan range, still covered with snow nearly to the base. This was the favourite summer residence of Yakub Beg. The remains of the fort where he lived, and which had been destroyed by the Chinese, were still visible. Passing through the *karaol* at the entrance of a fair-sized bazaar, we were now in the Ushturfan district, and reached the town itself in another day's journey.

The Amban of Aksu had sent word to the Chankoo, another name for the ruler of the district, announcing my visit. He sent out an Aksakal to escort me into the town, and conduct me to my place of residence—the usual Chinese pattern of guest-house, without either doors or windows, situated in a good-sized orchard.

Soon after, the Chankoo's Tunktchi appeared to announce that the great man would shortly pay me a visit. This was very civil, but rather a bore! In due time he drove up in his mule-cart, preceded by a band of curious instruments which made the most hideous noise. Going out to receive him, I handed him in. Fortunately he did not stay long, as he said he was ill, but begged me to ask for whatever I required. I told him all I wanted was a guide to show me where some shooting was to be had, and afterwards to put me on the way to Kashgar.

I had to remain a day to make arrangements, and was very glad to get these over and leave the place, being much bothered by Chinese visitors of the baser sort, who, with their usual intolerable curiosity, made themselves most objectionable.

Mahomed Amin, to see the last of me, accompanied me for a short distance outside the town. I was quite sorry to part with the old man; and when we bade each other adieu he was crying like a child, for he said he feared he would never see another Englishman.

Grass-prairies, varied with stony barren flats where the moraines came down from the hills on our left, was again the style of country, reminding me very much of the Taghdumbash

Pamir: it is very little cultivated, and inhabited entirely by Kirghiz.

Having done about twenty miles, we got to the camp of one Bash Agma, where my guide said a Beg resided who would be able to tell me where to look for goolja. The Beg was very civil, and gave me a little mud hovel to put up in, but could not give me much of the required information, as he said none of his people were shikaris. He had heard, however, that if I followed my present road up the Aksu river, which flowed through the valley, and then were to ascend the mountain-range to the left, I should find myself on a sort of table-land where it was reported poli were to be found; but at this season grass, water, and fuel were very scarce, and he did not think I should be able to remain.

Accordingly next day we followed the route he had indicated, the valley ascending gradually as we advanced. Snow-cocks and chikor were pretty numerous on the rocky slopes, though the altitude was only about 5000 feet, and I was surprised to find them at such a low level. Also coveys of partridges (*Perdrix barbatus*), which seem closely allied to ours. Of these I had already procured specimens, a cock and a hen, in Kalmuk. As yet there were no poli heads visible,—not that I expected to see them in the flesh so low down, but, as a rule, if any horned heads are to be got within carrying distance, they are to be seen on the *mazars* of the Kirghiz.

At a place called Safr Bai I met another Beg, but he could give me no authentic information either.

On reaching Soutan, some twenty miles beyond the last camp, my guide told me we were to leave the valley, turn up a nullah due south, and cross the range at whose base we had travelled the last three days. We tried to get information from the Kirghiz, but they appeared to know nothing.

Following the nullah at whose mouth we had camped, we ascended a gorge for about four miles: it was clad here and there with patches of low fir forest and juniper. Then passing over a col, we descended on to a sort of pamir.

Besides chikor and snow-cock, there were quantities of marmots. The hills on the south side of the range were covered with the fine pamir grass, so much prized for grazing purposes; but the Kirghiz did not seem to frequent this part, owing to the extreme scarcity of water.

Turning north up this pamir, we ascended another and higher pass of some 8000 feet. Beyond this was a table-land of about four miles, when we once more descended into a valley. The mountains, though fairly covered with grass, were without any springs; and we were very glad to catch sight of some *yurts* in the distance, just as it was getting dark, for it had been a long day — thirty miles or so — and not a drop of water on the road.

The mouth of this valley opened on to a pamir which looked very like poli-ground; but as the altitude was not more than 7000 feet, it seemed very improbable that they would be found there. I was therefore much astonished when a Kirghiz shikari rode up on a camel, and said he had heard I had come to hunt, and that if I pitched my camp at a water-channel a little way below, and remained a few days, he would show me some sport. Feeling utterly unbelieving, I said the only game one could expect on these low hills were jeran. Without a word he got off his camel, and from under the saddle produced the skin of an arkar or female *Ovis poli*, then said if I liked he would that very day take me to the spot where he had shot it a short time ago. I was bound to believe him, and when we got to the watercourse pitched the camp. It was a few miles from the shooting-ground, he said, but there was no water to be had nearer.

That afternoon I started with my new shikari to look for the promised poli. There were two ranges of hills between which the steppe extended, falling away from the greater or Ushturfan range in undulating hillocks, and cut up with a network of precipitous nullahs; amongst these my shikari said we would find our game. After going about eight miles we came to an open grassy hollow at the edge of the hillocks. Here we dismounted, I from my pony and the shikari from his camel; and being now at the shooting-ground, he said we had better hobble, and leave them until our return.

I confess to being still sceptical as to finding the poli so low down, but we had not gone a quarter of a mile when my doubts were dispelled: there, sure enough, were the tracks of a herd, and seemingly quite fresh. They were arkars certainly; but I made up my mind to shoot one, not having a female specimen, besides being in want of meat.

We followed the tracks along a gravelly ridge, keeping my rifle in hand, for such was the nature of the ground that there was a chance of coming across the herd at any moment. After walking about half a mile in this way, cautiously peeping round every corner, I thought I heard a movement in a ravine to my left. On looking over, there, sure enough, were half a dozen arkars taking their evening meal off the little tufts of grass which sprang through the gravel. Crawling cautiously down to within 100 yards, and selecting the easiest, a broadside shot, I fired. My bullet went thud into her shoulder, and over she went. The rest ran into a mob, and stood for a minute before making a rush, so that I could easily have shot another; but one being enough for my purpose, I let them be. Covering the carcass with some pieces of rock to keep the vultures off, we went on in the hopes of coming across a ram. There was another herd of arkars, but not a sign of a goolja to be seen—only one or two old heads lay about in the ravines. As evening was approaching, we turned our faces campwards, and next day moved my things to the Kirghiz camp, to be nearer my ground.

Taking Mahomed Atta and a couple of ponies, we returned to the ravine to bring in the Ovis, which we found all safe and unmolested by vultures or wolves. I could not see the slightest difference in this Ovis to that of the Pamirs, though it is distinguished by the name *Ovis Carolini.* No doubt it is found at a much lower altitude, as this steppe was barely 7000 feet above the sea; and it is quite possible that in the summer there may be a slight difference in the colour and length of the hair, but otherwise the two varieties appeared to be identical.

Having sent Mahomed off with the arkar to camp, I went farther on to look for a goolja, and after going a long way, saw one in the distance, but made out through the glasses that he was only a small one. Thinking that he was probably one of a herd on sentry-duty, I stalked him as soon as he moved on; but as I got over a brow of a hillock, he unfortunately saw me against the blue sky-line, and away he went. Following as fast as possible, I got within sight of the herd, a dozen small rams, but not a head amongst them worth a shot, so it did not signify.

Finding that my road to Kashgar took me over the head of this pamir, and feeling that it was not worth while to remain, being sure that there were no rams of any size in the neighbourhood, I sent my caravan on to a place called Pickand, and with the shikari hunted all the ground that lay between, but only saw two herds of arkars. There was no doubt, he said, a month earlier we should have fared better; but now the snow was melting the rams had moved off, in what direction he could not tell.

Making our way down the steppe towards evening, I saw a forest in the distance: this, my shikari said, was the camping-ground. The prospect of a plentiful supply of wood was a pleasant one, as the nights were still very nippy. Some Kirghiz came to visit me shortly after we got in, but did not appear to know much about the neighbourhood.

I had a stiff climb next morning on to the ridge, getting a most excellent view of the country round, if nothing else. To the south, away over the plains of Eastern Turkistan, were low ranges of rocky hills, each one perfectly parallel to the other, but not a sign of vegetation or water. These spurs were evidently quite barren, so there was nothing to be done but prepare for my next march, a long one of twenty-eight miles.

A great part of the way was by the edge of a lake, which in the distance appeared to be frozen over, but on nearer approach proved to be an immense salt-pan. Leaving this, we came to a most delightful little oasis called Jai Dubba. Here I pitched my tent, and found a spring of excellent water, with a group of poplars growing round. Hard by was a good-sized Kirghiz camp. The Beg was a very civil personage, bringing the usual presents of sheep, &c., which I returned with *chogas* and other small articles; but the thing of all others I most wanted—viz., information about sport—was unobtainable.

There was nothing for it but to resign the Carolini and get to Kashgar as soon as possible, to refit for a fresh expedition. The ponies had become very slack, and no wonder, considering they had been moving without intermission since the month of November. So turning my back to the mountains, I crossed the sandy steppe to a spring called Kyr Bulak. The sun was now beginning to make himself felt, and the heat off the sand made one long for an avenue of trees: still there was water, which was one thing to be thankful for, and the shade of my tent was another.

While meditating over my pipe that evening, and resting my somewhat wearied limbs, there suddenly came a whirr of wings overhead, and several grouse lighted by the spring to drink: they were the ordinary "Imperial grouse," such as are met with in the plains of North-West India in the cold weather. They are migrants, so probably came over these steppes.

Another rocky gorge brought us gradually down to a lower steppe, still more arid than the last, and from there the descent continued to a cultivated plain with villages and orchards. These scattered hamlets, which cover an area of from five to eight square miles, are called collectively Kalti Ailak.

We were now within a couple of marches of Kashgar,—the road being across this plain, past the village of Artish, which is of a considerable size, to a barren ridge of hill, the division between the valley of Artish and Kashgar. There was a very narrow defile through this ridge, being, in fact, a cutting with perpendicular sides, and so narrow that the ponies got jammed now and again with others coming the opposite way, retarding our progress very considerably. By slow degrees we got through, and as we emerged the country lay open beyond, and Kashgar was at our feet.

I had expected to find it a larger town, but it did not appear to be more than half the size of Yarkand. Entering the city by the east gate, and inquiring for the Russian Consulate, we found it was situated on the other side, outside the walls, so I rode straight through, intending to go and ask for news of Bower, who must have been there for some time: indeed my fear was that he might already have left, as his leave was nearly up. However, on getting to the other gate, I found he was still in the town, and living in a house close at hand.

CHAPTER X.

KASHGAR TO THE KARAART PAMIR.

THE CAPTURE OF DAD MAHOMED—EUROPEANS AT KASHGAR —A FRESH START—BY THE RIVER ULUART—ACROSS THE KOSH-BELI PASS—THE POLI DISAPPEAR—A LONG SHOT.

THERE is nothing more delightful than a meeting with a friend after a long lonely wandering in a strange country : the amount of news to be heard, the questions to be asked, and the notes that have to be compared, are matters of the deepest interest. To begin with, I was both astonished and delighted to hear that Dad Mahomed the murderer had been taken. Such a stroke of luck was most unexpected : although a rumour to that effect had reached me, it was so improbable that I did not believe it.

The capture was brought about in this way. After Bower and I had parted, he heard on reliable authority that Dad Mahomed had passed over the frontier into Russian Turkistan, and the idea was that he would go on from there to his native place, Kabul. He therefore sent one of his men off to Tashkurgan, where the Amir of Afghanistan then was, with the authority of the English Government to take him. The man had an interview with the Amir, who told him to search where he liked, he would not impede him, but that he did not think Dad Mahomed was in the country, which proved to be the case.

Another man, a moonshi in the service of the Government at Ladak, Shamshuddin by name, had been sent into Fargana to try and trace him there, and going over the frontier to Osh, he proceeded to Marghilan. There, hearing a rumour that the man had passed through that place on his way to Samarkand, the conjecture was that he had gone off to Mecca on a pilgrimage. It was the moonshi's last chance: if Dad Mahomed had gone to Mecca he would have reached it long since, and there would be no possibility of catching him. The moonshi therefore started immediately for Samarkand, and as he strolled through the bazaar the first day, whom should he see, to his intense astonishment, but the very man he wanted, disguised as a pedlar, sitting at a stall selling odds and ends.

The moonshi said that when he walked up to him he turned green with fright, and jumping up, looked like bolting. Shamshuddin made a sign to reassure him, and told him it was all right,—that he was no longer a servant of the Indian Government, having got into a row and bolted, like himself. (These two knew each other well at Leh.) After talking for some time, he said, "By the way, I have a packet of letters for you from your brother, who is now in Yarkand: I left them in the serai, and will go and fetch them for you."

Dad Mahomed got up as if to follow, but not liking to leave his wares, sat down again. The moonshi ran off to the Russian police-officer, and showing him his authority, begged him to take the man at once. The officer immediately ordered a file of police to follow Shamshuddin, who then returned to where he had left the villain, feeling a little uncertain as to whether he had not bolted in the meantime, but was delighted to find him still sitting tight; so walking up to him, he said, "Here are your letters," and then putting his hand on his shoulder, called out, "Dad Mahomed, murderer," on which the police pounced down and secured him before he had time to pull himself together. He was locked up in Samarkand, and then arose the question, What was to be done with him? The matter had been duly reported to the English and Russian Governments, and Bower was now waiting for orders. How long he would be kept was hard to say. The man would be sent back either through Russia or Chinese Turkistan, and, whichever way he went, Bower would have charge of him.

In the afternoon, Monsieur Teutsh, then acting as Russian Consul, and the Rev. Father Hendricks, a missionary who had resided in China and Mongolia for most of his life, came to call, and asked us over to the Consulate. There we met an officer of the Cossacks on guard at the Consulate, also a Polish gentleman who had taken up his residence at Kashgar. These formed the whole of the European society of the town.

We had a great talk in the evening over future proceedings. Bower was unfortunately tied by the leg until he got his orders, and even then shooting was out of the question for him; whilst I was very much divided in my own mind as to what I should do. In any case, I should return to the Pamirs for some more poli; but whether to return to India through Shighnan, Badakshan, and Chitral, or go to England *viâ* Russian Turkistan and the Caspian, that was the question.

I had made arrangements for a Russian passport before I left Kashmir, on the chance of wanting to follow the latter route, and whichever way I went, I should require another lot of ponies; so while making up my mind on the subject, I sent off Mahomed Atta to Yarkand with the present lot, and to bring back a fresh string of them in exchange. This would take him ten to twelve days. Meantime I intended to have a thorough rest and enjoy a little *dolce far niente*, feeling deservedly entitled to it after my winter's labours.

My tent was pitched in the garden of Bower's residence, on a platform under a grove of trees, an ideal place for a tent in hot weather, and for the first two days of my arrival it was so; but on the third day a violent dust storm blew up, followed by rain and thunder, which cooled the air considerably. Had it not been for the agreeable society of our friends at the Consulate, I must own we should have been bored to death. Excepting a ride in the morning, and a walk in the evening, our days were utterly without incident. Perhaps it was this that helped me to form my plans. The Russian route carried the day, by which I should reach England in July.

My idea was to start westward and get to the Pamirs by the Guz defile, and hunt for poli wherever the spirit might lead me, in the direction of the Great Kara-kul Pamir, dropping down by the Alai valley, and on to Marghilan, where I heard the post-road ran to Samarkand.

The ponies having arrived, and a Shighnani guide procured, who professed to know the country as far as the Russian frontier, I was once more in the saddle, getting to Borakatai, a distance of some twenty-five miles from Kaṣhgar, on the 10th of May. It was a large village, with well-cultivated land all round, which at this season gave the country a prosperous appearance, but which grew gradually less so, as our road led along the foot of the mountains, where the plains are always arid and stony. The day was so thick and hazy that we could see nothing of the mountains ahead; only a dimly formed outline was visible as we entered a bay between two stony spurs, the entrance of the Guz defile.

A short distance up the valley was a serai called Tash Balik, the custom-house or *karaol* for caravans coming from Badakshan and Shighnan.

Not wishing to overdrive the ponies at first, I put up there, and got a very good room.

Our start was rather retarded in the morning, owing to the heavy rain that had fallen throughout the night. Fortunately for us, as we had constantly to ford the river Uluart, the summer floods had not begun, and there was no very great difficulty. The road was a good flat one, and in excellent repair. Gradually the defile began to contract, the spurs on either side rising more and more precipitously. As the morning mists cleared off, occasional peeps were visible of the great snow-peaks of the Tagherma Mustagh range which we were to cross, and here and there before us were patches of fine forests. Bridges now became frequent, which were evidently kept up with some trouble, as they were all in good condition.

Following a zigzag course for about ten miles, we came to a jungly flat, where the guide advised a halt, grass and fuel being unobtainable for some considerable distance ahead; and as heavy ominous clouds were collecting on the mountains, and sundry claps of thunder warned us we were going to catch it, I was not sorry, and only just got my tent up in time, when down came the rain in perfect torrents. In a very few moments thousands of rivulets were pouring down over the rocks. The storm, fortunately for us, did not last throughout the night, and the morning broke clear and fine. The mountains looked very lovely, all freshly powdered with snow; and the gorge, as we advanced, became grand, the cliffs rising one above another right up to the snow : the air, too, had become crisp and cold. The road now began to be rough and stony, and the ups and downs over spurs which ran down to the river, where they ended in sharp cliffs, were frequent.

One of the ponies, out of pure devilment, took it into his head to try and ford the river when we were rounding one of these spurs, at whose base the road had been built up into a sort of causeway. The wretch, when about half-way round, quietly slipped off into the river, where the current immediately swept him off his legs and carried him down. Fortunately a turn below brought him back to our bank, and my men cleverly hauled him out. His load, luckily, was a light one, and well fastened to the pad : of course it was soaked through, but nothing was lost. This was fortunate, as it contained my *toshakarna—i.e.*, cotton prints, &c., to give away in exchange with the Kirghiz, and without which I should have been at a loss for supplies.

Once out of the defile, we were on the Pamirs again: here I came on a Kirghiz camp, and had some conversation with the Malik, telling him it was my intention to go to the Alichur Pamir for poli. He assured me it would be a very difficult journey, for the passes on the high range which lay between were still blocked with snow; "but," he continued, "as you are only going for sport, why not go on to Karaart, where there is plenty of goolja? The road is quite simple, and no passes to cross." This proposition was worthy of consideration, as, after all, there might be nothing to shoot there, while sport of some sort would be to be had on the Karaart; so I told him that I would take his advice if he could find me a guide. He immediately offered to come himself the first part of the way, and for the remainder it would be easy to procure another from one of the Kirghiz camps.

Having settled this matter, we turned our faces northward, and ascended the Uluart valley on the left bank of the river, along the base of the Tagherma Mustagh range. On the opposite side, to the westward, another range divided us from the Pamirs of Rangkul, Sariz, and Alichur.

The third day brought us to our camping-ground, a big flat, with good stretches of grass. There were three or four Kirghiz camps dotted about on the plain, amongst them that of the Malik, conspicuous by the large *yurt* in which he lived. The wind had been blowing a hurricane in our faces and was bitterly cold, so that I was very glad to accept his invitation and sit down in his dwelling until the caravan came up. We had a talk over the shooting on the Karaart, about which he said I had been misinformed. Formerly there were plenty poli, but an epidemic two years ago had cleared most of them off; the few that were left were always on the move, and very difficult to find. He gave me the name of a Kirghiz, Harim Khan, who knew the pamir well, and if any one could show me sport, he was the man to do it, and when I had had enough of that part, could conduct me over the pass to Karakul.

My things having now arrived, we pitched the camp hard by; but first had to attend to one of the ponies, who was in a very bad way, something having stuck in his throat too low down for me to get at. Unfortunately it was one of the best, a Kalmuki, a good willing beast, never sick or sorry. He died in the morning, much to the joy of the Kirghiz, who very soon cut him up and carried off the meat! I found a solid ball of grass had stuck at the base of the gullet. At the last camp a Kirghiz had given me some coarse dry stuff, and the poor animal, who was always ready for his food, had gone at it in too much of a hurry, and this was the result.

Getting to the head of this pamir, we crossed the Kosh-beli Pass, 15,500 feet, and gradually descended to a valley running down from the Karaart (black earth) range, which divided it from the Karakul Pamir.

My shikari took me to a grass flat where rather a rugged *yurt* was standing, the only occupant of which was a child of about six years old, who gave tongue lustily when we appeared at the door. It soon made friends, and the mother coming in, told us that her husband had gone off hunting, but would be back next day. There was not much, she said, to be had in the immediate neighbourhood, but higher up we should find more.

I was off before daylight, and got on to a

plateau cut up with numerous small ravines; but though we searched everywhere for tracks of poli for several miles round, none were to be found : the ground was utterly barren, not a blade of grass to be seen.

At the edge of this plateau we descended where one of the tributaries of the Markan-su or Kashgar river ran, following it up towards the Karaart mountains. Here we came across fresh tracks of poli, and about ten o'clock sighted the herd on a grass flat about a mile off. Had they remained there, it would have been an easy matter, but they shortly moved up to a gravel slope, and one after another lay down. I tried every possible way to get at them from below, but found it could not be done, and it was equally impossible to stalk them from above, as the wind was blowing straight down the valley. There was nothing for it but to follow their example, and lie down until it pleased them to move on to a more convenient ground for a stalk. Three mortal hours we lay and watched, until it was so cold I was obliged to move on, and determined to have one more try to circumvent them. My old shikari had gone to sleep, so I left him where he lay, proceeded up a water-course near where the herd had crossed, and looked cautiously over. To my horror not a vestige of them was to be seen! Something must have scared them, for I followed their tracks up the valley, crossing spur after spur, expecting every moment to see them; but at last had to give it up, the tracks showing they had gone over the main divide between this and the next valley. This was too far to venture without a guide, especially as the day was waning.

When I got back to where the old shikari was lying asleep, he was nowhere to be seen: there was nothing for it but to sling my rifle on my back and tramp home alone, and getting on to my tracks, I followed them down to camp, where I expected to find him in before me. Nothing, however, was heard of him either that night or next morning, and I began to get alarmed; but a Kirghiz, who lived in a *yurt* near, thought it was most probable he had gone on to where his brother dwelt in the next valley. To my great relief, I met him on the road. He said he had lost me the day before, though he had hunted about everywhere until dark: finally coming across a *yurt*, he spent the night there.

Feeling desperately bloodthirsty, I determined to go back to the place where I originally saw the herd, and had not left camp an hour before we came upon them face to face, just emerging from some broken ground about 200 yards from where we were. Fortunately the first goolja was looking the other way, and down we dropped on to the stones like logs. One by one they came in sight, just too far to make a certain shot. I neither moved a muscle nor winked an eye, hardly even breathed. On they came filing past, still keeping the same distance, rather over 200 yards.

Now that I had a good view of their heads, they were rather disappointing: distance, as usual, had lent enchantment, — they were not so large as could have been wished. For a short time not one of them noticed us as they pottered along grazing, but at last one of them threw up his head and looked at us fixedly. Would he make us out or not? A terrible moment of suspense ensued. Presently he gave a stamp with his foot and the usual note of alarm. Instantly every head was thrown up. It was a case of now or never. Sitting up, I covered what appeared to be the best one, right in the middle. I felt pretty steady, but the distance was greater than I thought: the bullet went under him, striking a stone and knocking up the dust, then went pinging away beyond. I gave them the other barrel as they ran, but with no result. Away they went without a pause, until they appeared like specks against the sky.

This seemed to be the only herd in the district, so I determined to waste no more time, but go on to the Karakul Pamir.

CHAPTER XI.

THE KARAKUL PAMIR—AND HOME.

IN RUSSIAN TERRITORY—A STERN CHASE—FOUND DEAD—HARD HIT—AN ICE RAFT—FINISHED AT LAST—A WILD LOT—AN ADVENTUROUS LADY—WE LOSE THE CARAVAN—A SAD PARTING—THE TENGIZ-BAI PASS—AT THE CUSTOM-HOUSE—A RIDICULOUS MISTAKE—MARGHILAN—BREAKING UP THE CARAVAN—JOURNEY BY *TARANTASS*—RETURN TO CIVILISATION.

RETRACING our steps to the last camp, we turned up a valley due west, which led down from the Karaart Pass, and camped on a flat place at sundown. There was sufficient grass to amuse the ponies; of fuel there was none. Fortunately we had taken the precaution to bring on a sack of cow's dung, which sufficed for culinary purposes.

Once across the Karaart Pass, which is 15,800 feet, we were in Russian territory. The ascent was easy enough, but the ponies felt the altitude. The top of the pass was flat, with about 2 feet of soft snow upon it.

From here there was a beautiful view of the Karakul Pamir, with the great salt lake of that name in the centre. It was still frozen over in the eastern portion; but the western, which is nearly cut off by two promontories, was open water, and of an intense blue colour. To the north, running east and west, extended the Trans-Alai mountains, with Kaufmann Peak towering head and shoulders above the rest, looking splendid with his great snowy cap. The cold, however, was too intense to linger long even over such a magnificent scene as this; so we set to work to zigzag our way from the crest by a pretty steep descent to the valley which led to the Khargoshi Pamir.

There we saw a group of *yurts* in the distance, in one of which, my old shikari said, we should probably find Karim Khan. Riding up to the best of these, I asked a Kirghiz standing near if Karim Khan lived there? "No," he replied; "he has gone off to Karaart with some sheep."

This was rather a bad shot, as we had just come from there, and I told him so. "Oh, if he has not gone there, he has gone elsewhere," was the calm reply.

I was rather disappointed to hear this, as the Beg at Karaart told me he was a very good shikari—in fact, the only one in that part; so I offered the man a suitable reward to find him for me.

At this moment up comes my old shikari, and embraces him warmly! I told him Karim Khan was away. "Oh no," he said; "*this* is Karim Khan!"

Most people would have looked rather foolish at being caught out in such a manner: not so Mr Karim Khan, who did not even take it as a joke, but looked as solemn as a judge.

On my asking why he had told such a deliberate falsehood, when I had no wish to harm him, but, on the contrary, would pay him well if he would go with me for a few days' shooting, he said he was afraid I might be angry with him if the sport was not good : there were some gooljas about, but it was quite impossible to say where they would be found.

After a little talk we got quite friendly, and he agreed to hunt with me on the mountains beyond the camp, and then to go round by the west of the Karakul; only he begged me to remember that big heads were very scarce, and not to be angry if I only got small ones. Accordingly we started early up the stony slope, until we came to the top of a ridge about five miles off, and on looking over, an enormous corrie opened before us, where the shikari said he expected to find the herd; and, sure enough, there they were, feeding on a patch of grass right in the centre. A more impossible place for a stalk I never saw: the corrie was exactly like half a teacup, without a scrap of cover. There was nothing for it but to play the waiting game, and see where they went; but the cold became intense, and as they were evidently settled for the day on a place after their own hearts, with water, grass, and nice soft gravel to lie on, we gave it up, intending to return in the evening, but the snowstorms came on so frequently that I put off until the morrow.

They were still there when I got back, only a little lower down, poking away in the fresh snow to get at the grass. At length they moved on towards the ridge on the opposite side of the corrie. As the last white stern disappeared from view, I started in pursuit. Though the distance looked short, it was a good mile across, and looking over, not a sign of them was to be seen. At that moment the shikari, grasping my arm, pointed upwards. There they were ascending another corrie just above. Following on, we got up to their level on the other side, and looked over again. Bad luck to it, there they were walking along just out of shot! Yet another long wait. This time, when their heads disappeared (for I could not wait for the tails), we were after them, cocking my rifle as I went, feeling sure we should catch them this time; but not a bit of it. *Excelsior* was evidently their motto that day. Karim Khan said if I wished it we could follow, but as there was no more grass, they were not likely to stop until they were over the top of the mountain and down the other side.

At daybreak I was up, intending to make a move to the west side of the Karakul; but my rascally ponies upset my plans, as they were nowhere to be found, and the men had to go in all directions before they could be collected.

We had rather a dreary march, but found a good place to set up house, with patches of grass and plenty of water and *burtsa*. Given some game on the hills, there was nothing more to be desired.

We came on a herd in much the same kind of ground as had already baffled me, but at last we managed to make out a line behind a slight swell on the surface, down which I went on my back feet foremost, inch by inch, to where I had marked them. Casting one eye over cautiously, I just made out the top of a horn, and seeing a friendly stone a little farther below, worked my way gradually there, putting it between myself and the outside head, and from behind its shelter got a view of the entire herd, nine of them all told. They were lying chewing the cud about 120 yards away. I looked them carefully over to select the best head, but as he was not in a position to shoot at, I had to lie still until he pleased to move. Presently one got up and stretched himself broadside on to me, a lovely shot; but he was not the one on which my affections were set. Two or three others did the same, and after scraping a hole in the gravel lay down again. At last my ram got on his legs and looked down the slope, away from me; after a bit, round he came. Now was my chance! I was up in an instant, and just had the bead on his shoulder when up got another and covered him. The brute! I felt much inclined to shoot him, only he was a small one. At last my friend walked forward. The moment he showed clear of the other I fired: the bullet went thud into his ribs, but he was away with the rest. As they went off I shot another, knocking him head over heels like a rabbit, but he was on his legs in a minute and joined the herd.

As there was a good extensive view from my present position, I sat still and watched them with the glasses. Number one had lagged all the way, and when the herd turned off to the left below, he kept on to the right, going over a low spur. The second one that had been knocked over was not to be distinguished as he ran with the rest, so I concluded he had been shot high on the shoulder, probably only grazing the withers.

The herd now being out of sight, we followed as fast as possible on their track. My shikari presently pointed out that they had turned up the hill, evidently with the intention of crossing the range. Clapping the glasses on them, I saw eight still to the fore, which included the second one wounded. As they were going strong, I gave them up as a bad job, and turned back to finish the first one, fancying it would be an easy matter. On crossing the spur over which he had disappeared, we got on to a broad table-land about a couple of miles across, and right in the middle could distinguish the goolja walking slowly along.

This was rather a sell, as we had expected to find him dead, or at all events the next thing to it. There was blood on his track, but not much, so the only thing for it was a stern chase. We soon lost sight of him, and had to set to work and track. He led back towards the camp—a capital move, if only he would stop and let me finish him. When we came again within sight, he was crossing an open corrie, so we had to wait until he had left it, then run hard to try and get a shot; but it was no go, he was again out on the open. Here he lay down, but with his head well up, quite on the look-out. There was only one way to stalk him, by making a long detour and trust to his remaining meanwhile.

Getting at last round on to the ridge, I worked down on my back over the gravel slope, until his horns came within sight some 200 yards below. Feeling it would be well to make certain of him, I continued my descent, when suddenly he got up, and as he stood, got a good view of me as I lay. Away he went best pace, too far for a running shot, and both barrels missed him clean. The red patch of my first bullet was plainly visible in the middle of his body : it was surprising how strong he went with such a wound.

There was nothing for it but to follow. The tracks led straight towards my camp, and actually right up to within 50 yards of my tent. The servants said that as he trotted quietly past them they saw the wound, and expected every moment to see him drop as he ascended the slope. As he had gone up the hill, and we were at the camp, and the hour barely eleven o'clock, I determined to fortify myself with a good breakfast before resuming the chase.

In half an hour we were at it again, the ram keeping steadily on without the smallest symptom of giving in. Spur after spur we crossed, always ascending, until at three o'clock we were right on the top of the range and looking down on the Khargoshi Pamir, with the Muskol or Ice lake on the other side. The blood-tracks, which had been getting scanty, at last disappeared, and I realised that there was nothing for it but to return to camp. It was a grievous disappointment, but the day was waning and the distance to cover considerable ; also my shikari complained of feeling unwell, and could go no farther. Sadly and reluctantly we retraced our steps. Verily *Ovis poli* are the strongest beasts when wounded I ever had to do with.

Trying the same nullah next morning, we sighted a herd of eight in a corrie above, where we found some the day before. To get at them it was necessary to make a long round, and during my absence five of these had cleared off. It was impossible to do anything until the remainder followed, and as soon as these were out of sight we resumed the stalk, which was of a similar nature to that already described : a slither down on my back, then a longish wait for the best one to get up and give me a fair shot. But my anguish may be imagined, when he did get up at 150 yards, and, although steady and careful, I missed him clean ! Whether the shot went over or under his body it is hard to say—probably over, for it was a steep down-hill shot.

Furious with myself, my inclination was to break the rifle in two. The shikari and Mahomed Atta came up and tried to console me ; but after yesterday's luck it was hard lines, besides the feeling of missing before natives, who have such an exalted opinion of our weapons. However, in a measure this disgrace was wiped out at once ;

for as we stood talking, a little marmot about the size of a rabbit sat up on end, just where the Ovis had stood. Pointing him out to the shikari, and telling him to watch where the bullet struck the ground, so as to prove whether it was a misjudged distance, I fired again, without the least expectation of hitting so small an animal; but, to my great satisfaction, he tumbled over, and on going to him I found the bullet had blown his head and shoulders clean off.

Having worked right round the group of hills, and seen nothing but some ewes and small rams, I moved my camp on about ten miles across the Karakul Pamir to a range of hills east of the lake, where, after pitching my tent and having breakfast, I started with the determination to bag something. As we went along, four *Ovis poli* crossed our path; but they saw us, and went on across the valley. The wind was blowing up the *jilgas*, as the nullahs are called in Turki, so I made for the main ridge, thus getting the wind in my favour, to work down on anything I might find.

In the middle of the second corrie there was a good herd, but they lay in a perfectly open place, with no means of approach. However, they could not lie there for ever, so the next best thing was to get as near as possible, preparatory to a move on their part. As we were working round the corrie, they began to walk towards the side we were making for, so we ran along quickly to circumvent and meet them on the shoulder. On getting there, we found them still in the corrie, and an undulation in the ground gave me the chance of a similar stalk to my last—viz., by sliding down on my back to a distance of 150 yards, with the herd below me, some feeding, some lying down. I meditated taking a shot, but thinking there was a possibility of getting closer, went crawling on to a little ridge of stones below, when the warning note sounded, and the whole herd were on their feet with one bound! My move was a false one, having gone a little too low, and they had got my wind. There was no time for deliberation, so, sitting up, I fired at a ram with a decent head; and as they made off across the corrie, I gave my left barrel to another, which smashed his thigh.

As soon as they disappeared we were after them. Unfortunately, the next corrie was an open one, and on looking into it, we saw the wounded rams lying one on each side, making it impossible to try for one without showing myself to the other. It was very perplexing to know what to do. Evening was closing in; it was not likely they would go far, and one would probably die in the night. Whilst debating over this, one got up and walked across to the other. Thinking there was now a chance of circumventing them from above, I went round the top of the corrie and down part of the way; but by this time it was getting too dark to see them distinctly, and I decided, rather than risk disturbing them to no avail, to go back to camp and return in the morning.

We were up there early; but they were earlier still, and had both disappeared. Their tracks showed that they had left their corrie and crossed the plain below to the opposite hills, about a mile off. There we discovered one of them lying in a ravine pretty high up, which gave on to the plain. The other was nowhere to be seen.

As the wind was blowing up-hill, there was nothing for it but to go upwards and get above my beast. We had not gone 500 yards when there were tracks of blood about, and a little beyond lay the missing Ovis stone dead. This was encouraging, so we continued after the other one, having marked the place very carefully beforehand; but on reaching the ravine not a trace of him was visible. Close by was another little nullah: if he was lying in this, it would be an easy stalk. Cautiously crawling along to the edge, I looked over, and there he was standing, 25 yards off, looking me straight in the face! As he was so near, it was not necessary to wait for him to turn, so I aimed at his chest, and the deed was done.

Leaving Karim Khan in charge of the dead, I set off along the range in the hope of getting another chance on my homeward way, but had no further luck, and on getting in sent the ponies to bring back the slain.

The following day we sighted another herd, but could not come within shot of them. When at the top of the valley where we had been the day before, we found it well stocked, there being several herds of ibex and arkars, but not a head amongst them worth shooting; so we turned off to a *jilga* due east of the camp, and at the head of this found another herd of ibex, but no good heads. Crossing over the ridge into the valley beyond, which ran due south, we discovered a good herd of rams. Again their position necessitated a long stalk, ending in a very steep ravine. On peeping round a corner, what should I see but the head of an Ovis looking over the edge of the cliff about 400 yards above me, on the opposite side! Presently he turned and walked out of sight. No sooner had he disappeared before another turned up, and soon the whole herd was on the move. If they came my way, it would be all right; but if they went up the hill, they would be placed, as it were, in a teacup, and quite unapproachable.

Being amongst some rocks at an angle giving a good view, besides affording cover, I remained there and watched the sky-line. They were evidently grazing their way down, and in my direction, for once in a way coming to be shot. First one showed himself opposite, and came over into my ravine, and then was followed by some of the others. They were sportively inclined, and butted at each other as they pottered along, scratching their backs against the rocks like sheep. They came exactly in front of where I lay, fearing almost to breathe. Still, although within 150 yards, I did not shoot, having seen some better heads above, and waited for the whole herd to come into view, so as to select the best head before firing. The rest, however, did not follow, and these few rejoining the others, the whole herd disappeared once more.

Rushing down the slope, scrambling up the other side, hard on their tracks, I lay panting on the crest. There were the whole herd, consisting of about a dozen, in full view. While getting my wind, I scanned them carefully. As usual, the best heads were the farthest away. Having pulled myself together, I selected one, about 130 yards off, broadside on. As luck would have it, just as the sight was well on to him, he turned round a little my way; but feeling pretty sure, I pulled the trigger. Away they rattled as hard as they could lay legs to the ground, excepting the one fired at, who stood for a moment as if stunned. Every instant I expected to see him drop: instead of this, he recovered himself and made off slowly after the rest. I gave him the other barrel, but he continued his journey on three legs!

There was no other chance at the herd, as they went right across the corrie without pausing a second. Being pretty sure of the beast, I did not trouble myself to follow in a hurry, thinking that if left alone he would probably lie down. But when he disappeared over a spur we felt it was time to start, and were surprised to see him keeping on at a steady pace. The prospect of a stern chase was not encouraging. Where could the first bullet have struck him? There was plenty of blood on the track, so there was not much fear of losing it.

Previous experience had taught me what a difficult beast to catch a wounded goolja is, but my wildest dreams had never conceived what it is possible for them to do until following this one. He went away down the slopes, stopping every now and again to look about, leaving lots of blood on his trail. Twice we nearly caught him, but on each occasion only saw his head, so I could not shoot. On and on he went over the spurs, and at last, leaving the hill, descended to the flat pamir below. It was getting on for afternoon, and he had vanished out of sight!

About half a mile from the hills was the river: here was a stumper. The edges were frozen on both sides, with an interval of deep running water about 20 yards wide in the centre. The trail showed that the plucky animal had swum across this, so follow we must. Karim Khan said it was impossible: it certainly looked rather like it, and I began to fear we were done, for the water was too cold to swim,—visions of cramp floated before me,—when suddenly an inspiration flashed into my mind as a piece of ice came floating along on our side, of about 8 to 10 yards square,—if it was thick enough it would bear us over! I chanced it, and jumping on as it came by, shouted to my shikari to follow quickly, which he promptly did, and we sailed quietly down the stream. As it twisted about, it was not long before the current swung us across to the opposite side. This came off quicker than we expected, and as soon as there was a chance we jumped on to the ice-edge, which gave a great crack as we landed, but fortunately held.

Taking up the track again, we made out our beast, after a little while, ascending the lower slopes of the opposite hill. He did not go very far up before halting, and then lay down. The wind, unfortunately, was blowing down the mountain, and though we tried every way to get at him from below, it was no good,—he quite commanded the situation.

Evening was coming on, and it was not probable, if left alone, that he would go far in the night, whereas, if scared, he might go anywhere, so we decided to leave him quiet and return in the morning. Fortunately, we found a place where the river was frozen over, and had not to risk an ice-raft again, which, however well it served our turn, is scarcely to be recommended as a permanent mode of conveyance. We were then good six miles from camp, and only just got back before dark.

Away again, nothing daunted, we went at daybreak to the spot where we had left the wounded creature—not a sign of him to be seen! There was nothing for it but to set to work and track again. We found the place where he had evidently laid up for the night; but thinking he must be stiff and not far away, I proceeded very cautiously, rifle at the ready, in case of coming on him suddenly. Whilst we were popping about amongst the rocks in the ravine, some stones rattled down from the steep hill above. There, sure enough, was a beast making his way along, but surely not my three-legged one? How could he have climbed so high? Turning the glasses on to him, the question was quickly solved; it was the wounded ram, and going apparently as strong as ever! Did the brute never mean to stop? Going along the face of the cliff, he turned up a narrow steep rift, and after looking about a little, lay down. The wind now blew up-hill, so needs must that I should climb the hill and descend

R

upon him. This was rather a difficult business, having to go round the hill out of sight, and yet get well above his level.

On getting round, he had disappeared again. Could he have moved? It was not possible to see quite to the bottom of the water-course, and if the Ovis lay in it, he would be out of my sight until walking right on to him. To make sure, the shikari went above to see if his tracks showed as having gone over the top, which was not far from where we were. He had gone no distance before he came slithering back in great excitement, having spotted the goolja in the water-course below. He showed me the exact spot, so I started off as quickly as the nature of the ground would permit. It was very steep, and here and there slopes of loose shale had to be avoided. Nearer and nearer I got to the spot where he lay, until I at last reached the edge of the watercourse, which was about eight feet deep, and was just crawling on, when I heard my friend get up, and the stones rattled down the nullah. There was a pause. Up came a head, and then a body, within ten yards of me. A bang, a crash, and over he went head over heels, shot through the heart and finished at last!

My first bullet had caught him on the horn, and just saved his shoulder, as he turned at the moment of firing; the second struck him on the haunch and smashed his thigh.

The head was not large, measuring about 50 inches; but it was a very effective one, spreading out well, and looking much bigger than it really was.

There were no more animals on this range. We therefore prepared to move on towards Alai, which is on the other side of Kara-kul, and thus on my homeward route.

From where we were the line to be taken was by the Kizil Art Pass, so sending the camp on in that direction, I proceeded myself in search of further spoil. I came across a herd, but could not get on terms with them: something must have scared them,—they were thoroughly unsettled. So I tried again the following day, and found my friends about ten miles away, feeding in the grassy bottom of a deep ravine. It was not an easy stalk, the wind being in the wrong direction, and I had to go a long way up the sky-line before a descent could be made upon them. At last getting into the watercourse where they were, and crawling cautiously round a spur which concealed the spot, I managed after some little time to distinguish a few in a depression among the rocks. Presently another head appeared, and crawling on a little farther, we saw them all lying about 120 yards off. The cover of stones was very scanty, so I dared not raise my head for a full view, knowing that, had they but a glimpse of it, they would be up and away; so I got my rifle ready, and prepared to shoot the first with a good head that gave me the chance. I had not long to wait before one was on his legs, but tail on to me. His horns seemed to stick out well, so I decided to shoot the moment he turned. He walked on, taking a bite here and there, carefully keeping his tail in my direction. At last he turned and scratched his ear with his hind-leg, and as he did so my bullet plugged into his ribs.

Preparing to take a shot at another, I waited for them to make the usual pause after a spurt up-hill; but they were a real wild lot, evidently knowing what a shot meant, and never stopped a second. There was nothing for it but to chance a couple of running shots at two others, who had been a little apart, as they sprang up the hill to join the rest. However, it was to no purpose, for they were well out of range. My other shot had told true, and the Ovis was quite dead; so we cut off his head, and covering the body for Karim Khan to pick up on his way back next day, started off to look for the camp.

A long cold tramp we had with the wind in our teeth, and it was a real luxury to find my tent pitched, and have a cup of tea. After which, feeling fit for anything, and a Kirghiz woman bringing news of a *Faringhi* who had crossed the Alai and was camped near, I was off like a shot, for the prospect of a talk with a fellow-creature was too good to be neglected. It was beginning to get dusk, and not a sign of a camp was to be seen, and I was reluctantly going to return, when, on crossing a spur, I came on a couple of *yurts*, and standing in front of one was a white man. This turned out to be Mr Littledale, who had been on this pamir and shot some poli the year before. Mrs Littledale was with him, and they told me they intended to try and work back to Kashmir *viâ* Badakshan and Chitral,—a very venturesome journey for a lady to take, and from which project I endeavoured to dissuade them, telling them that by all accounts the fords in Chitral were deep and dangerous at this time of year, and that they ran a good chance of losing their luggage. They had made up their minds, however, and there was nothing more to be said; so I was very glad to hear afterwards that they had got through all right.

The descent from the Kizil Art pass into the Alai valley was a most delightful change. Such a relief, after these great desert pamirs, to come upon a wide open valley of undulating prairies covered with beautiful green grass, and here and there a sign of human habitation, even though it was only a Kirghiz *yurt!* These, as yet, were few and far between, this being the summer residence of the Kirghiz from the Farghana (Russian Turkistan), and only a small number had arrived.

Once on to the prairie, we had the greatest difficulty in keeping the ponies going: they had their noses into the grass every minute, and no wonder, poor beasts! considering what scanty fare they had had latterly. But they gave me just cause for complaint next morning, when we woke up, to find that although they had plenty of grass under their noses, they must needs go and look for it elsewhere. Every one of them had taken French leave, excepting my two riding-ponies, which were picketed. We had to search in all directions, and it was mid-day before we succeeded in collecting the party—a *ruse*, no doubt, on their part, to curtail the day's march. They made up for it on the morrow, though in a way as little expected as intended, and which came about in this manner.

Having forded the Kizilean river, we proceeded down the right bank. The road so far was good and flat, and although somewhat undefined in places, there was no chance of losing our way. It had snowed a good deal the previous day; this morning, however, broke clear and bright. The snow in the valley had melted as it fell, though on the surrounding mountains it lay thick. Very grand they looked in their mantle of white—a splendid contrast and background to the broad green valley. At about four o'clock, being a mile or two ahead of the ponies, I began to look about for a convenient camping-ground, and selected a nice grass flat, with plenty of dry cow-dung scattered about for fires.

There were some natives on the road, who told me that a Kirghiz camp was to be found somewhere near, so thought it as well to take a look round a spur which led down to the river from the hills, on which there was a path, to see if they were anywhere about, in which case we could camp with them, and if not, take the spot already selected. It took me rather longer to get round the spur than I anticipated, and my labour was in vain, there being no signs of a camp beyond, so I retraced my steps. What was my surprise, on looking across the plain for the caravan, to find that not a vestige of them was to be seen, although from the spur there was a clear view of at least four miles between it and the next ridge. Concluding something must have happened to stop them, I got on my pony and galloped back. Still not a creature was visible, and a heavy shower of sleet coming on, prevented my seeing any distance beyond.

It was not possible to tell from the tracks whether they had passed or not, owing to numerous other marks of Kirghiz who had been passing during the day. Presuming they must have gone on, and crossed the spur instead of following my path by the river, I rattled back to my guide —who, by the way, knew nothing of the country —and Jaffer, both of whom had remained on the spur meanwhile.

Matters were assuming a serious turn; for

darkness was coming on rapidly, and there seemed a very good chance of spending the night in the open without food or blankets. The caravan by that time must have got a good start of us, and would go wandering on, thinking we were ahead; and once night closed in, there was no possibility of finding them. Telling my men there was nothing for it but to do our utmost to catch them up, I put Jaffer on my pony, as my walking powers as regards pace were much better than his, and the guide being mounted, we started off at the double, determined to make a race for it. Darker it grew and darker. Every now and then we stopped, gave a halloa, and then ran on. At last, to our relief, came an answering shout, and after a short distance we caught up the caravan, which was wandering aimlessly on in search of us.

There was no possibility of selecting a camp, being already quite dark, and unfortunately we were on a stony part of the plain. However, after groping about a little, we found sufficient *burtsa* to make a fire to cook with, and there was water in the river; but not a blade of grass for the ponies—a just retribution for them: not that they were starved, as there fortunately remained a good supply of grain.

At this period there came a very sad parting. I had decided to send back Rahimdar, the Kashmiri cook, and my excellent four-footed friend Joker—the former to Kashmir, and the latter to Monsieur Teutsh at the Consulate in Kashgar. Fitting out the *chef* with all the requisites for his journey, and giving him one of the ponies to ride and carry his kit, I told him to go back with a guide who knew the road to Kashgar, where he would probably find Captain Bower, and return with him to Kashmir: failing that, there would no doubt be a chance with some other caravan, to which he could attach himself. It was a most touching farewell, and the poor dog evidently grasped the situation, for on bidding him good-bye he set to work to howl as if his heart would break. The Kashmiri joined in, and I left them singing in chorus.

To say that my feelings were harrowed is no word for it; and as I went sorrowfully on my way, I missed my faithful companion of all these months more than can be expressed, and would have given anything that night to have seen him come trotting back into my tent.

Our start had been somewhat late, in consequence of this separation; we therefore made a short march, and camped near some Kirghiz *yurts* in order to get a guide to take me over the Tengiz-bai Pass to the Russian *karaol* on the other side of the Alai mountains.

The path up the precipitous glen was rough and stony, and wound about a good deal, the stream having constantly to be forded; but by mid-day we reached the summit, 11,800 feet. There was no view of the Farghana plain to be obtained, the distance being blocked by snow-peaks and rocky crags at every point. The ascent had been fairly easy, but the descent was more trying. Now and again there were some flat places, but more frequently the path pitched down through very abrupt moraines of stones and rocks. The bridges fortunately were good and firm, and, generally speaking, the path was much better looked after and kept in repair than our own road over the Karakoram from Ladak.

This pass is the highroad from the Russian Farghana to the Alai, and every year, and, by bad luck, just at this season, caravan after caravan of Kirghiz come trooping up with their herds to the fine grazing-grounds in the valley of that name. The path was only about as wide as a table in many places, and sometimes cut along the precipitous sides of the glen, with a fall of 1000 feet into the river below. Of course in the worst places there was always a caravan, and then would ensue a terrible jumble, for the great awkward camels are very difficult to steer in a narrow place; and as these caravans came at intervals of half a mile all day long, my progress, had I halted for each, would have been far from rapid. Getting rather desperate, I conceived the plan of keeping a man ahead as advance-guard, and he stopped the camels in convenient places where we could pass. Their drivers were uncommonly civil, and never refused to wait.

When we came to a flat piece of ground we were glad to pitch the tents, for it had been a tiring march for man and beast. There was a little dry wood about for kitchen purposes, but no grass. The hungry sheep and goats of the Kirghiz had eaten every blade as they passed by.

The next day was a repetition of what we had already gone through—Kirghiz sheep and goats everywhere; but by evening we came in sight of a mud house on a grass flat, which was the *karaol*. Near it were a few hamlets and some fields of Indian corn and lucerne, the first signs of civilisation. There were two customs-officers, one of them being Russian, who with many apologies asked to see my passport and to examine my goods, in which he had a right-down good worry, impounding a few cotton handkerchiefs, to which I made him very welcome, having no further use for them myself! It was a relief to find my gun and rifles were not questioned at all.

The temperature that evening was charming. We had descended to a level of about 5000 feet; and the softness of the air was very grateful after the biting cold on the high ranges.

Passing Uch Kurghan, at the mouth of the valley, the plains of Farghana at last came in sight, and I realised the final pass was crossed, and the next day would be spent in a Russian cantonment. The caravan would be dismissed, and, what seemed still more odd, I should be travelling off to Europe in a post-chaise!

This plain is very similar to the plains of Chinese Turkistan—the same irrigated cultivated flats, broad stony steppes, and undulating sandhills.

It was a good twenty-five miles to Marghilan, and the rain began to fall soon after our start, so that by the time we arrived we were soaking wet. On entering the town, Jaffer inquired for the rest-house, as I felt diffident of making use of a letter of introduction given me by Monsieur Teutsh at Kashgar. A large bungalow was pointed out, which looked thoroughly deserted; but there was a smaller house in the compound which seemed inhabited, and after some hammering a boy came out and said no one was in. Through Jaffer I informed him this was a lie, as it was the public rest-house, and as travellers we required accommodation. A very sleepy, sulky-looking Sart, as the people are called in these parts, came out at this point of the proceedings, and said this was his private house, and asked what the —— I meant by disturbing him. Being cross, hungry, and wet, my reply was made in choice Hindustani, which he understood to a certain extent; then remounting, I turned my back and rode away.

After wandering about, looking in vain for the rest-house, I thought, after all, it would be just as well to make use of my letter of introduction, and showing the address to the first decent-looking man, I was directed back to the very house from which we had been ejected! This was indeed a joke. We inquired for the owner, giving the boy, who appeared to be his servant, the letter. In a moment out came my friend, Atta Khan by name, and asked why the letter had not been given to him before; so I explained that we had laboured under a most ridiculous mistake, having taken the house for a post-house, while he took me for a loafer. He then showed me into his best apartment, made me his guest, and placed a horse and carriage at my disposal.

Marghilan is very much like our Indian cantonments in Lower Bengal, having fine trees, shrubberies, and gardens, throughout which are detached bungalows. But here the similarity ends, for when strolling round the public gardens in the evening, scarcely a soul was to be seen, only a few Russian officers strutting about in uniform. There was no polo, no racquet-court, no cricket, or officers hammering about the roads in flannels and blazers, or any of that cheery life that marks a British quarter, and makes banishment tolerable.

Having paid my respects to the head of the police, shown him my Russian passport, and asked for a permit to travel by post to Samarkand, he civilly assured me that this passport would take me anywhere without any trouble in Russia.

The next move was to settle my affairs, and break up the caravan, sending most of my camp kit and things back to Yarkand by Mahomed

Atta as a present to Mahomed Unis, who had found me in ponies during my stay in the country; then to pay off every one except Jaffer, whom I determined to take on to Samarkand, leaving my riding-pony with Atta Khan for him to ride back to Ladak.

Bidding my kind host adieu, we got into the *tarantass* or post-chaise, and started at eight o'clock for Khokand. The road was very bad, but the three ponies whisked along at a capital pace, covering the fifty miles by three o'clock.

Khokand is a large native city, with a fine bazaar, and there is a small Russian cantonment outside the walls; but it has the melancholy air which all cities of the past seem to assume.

The heat on the road and the dust were frightful, making me feel the sooner this part of the journey was got over the better; so we pushed on twenty miles farther to Bish-arik, where there was a post-house, but no kitchen and no bed, so we had to make the best of some food we had with us, and sleep on the floor.

Khojend was the next stage, and from there to Ura-Tapa, where the Russian in charge of the post-house was most civil and obliging, providing me with a breakfast and dinner of the usual

Russian type; and at 8 P.M. I was off once more, thinking the drive in the cool of the evening would be enjoyable. And so it was at first, but when nature began to assert herself, and sleep stole upon me, it was not so pleasant being jerked and jolted until my head seemed likely to part from my body. But, in spite of this discomfort, I persevered on my way until midday brought us to Jizak.

After all the heat and dust a tub would have been very refreshing, and though I had my folding bath with me, the post-house was so crammed with people that there was not a corner in which to take it.

A short rest and some food, and by sunset we were on the road again, being determined to get to Samarkand the next day if possible, and though there was a stoppage of two hours at Ak-Tapa, we succeeded in reaching it at 11 A.M. Here we drove through the native city by a good road to the Russian cantonments, and were directed to a fairly comfortable hotel, where I was treated in a half-European, half-Oriental manner. It was a luxury to have a few bodily comforts after the heat and dust of the way, and a rest of two days was by no means amiss. By that time the mail-train, which leaves twice a-week for Osonada on the shores of the Caspian, was due to start.

The journey by rail occupied two days and three nights. The line appeared well laid, and the Oxus bridge to be solid enough; but it was so hot and dusty that it was impossible to see much of the country we passed through.

The change to sea-breezes on board a good ship was very welcome, especially as it was a comfortable British-built steamer. We reached Baku the next morning. From there to Batoum was a journey of thirty hours *viâ* Tiflis, after which the line was pleasant and interesting, being over the lower ranges of the Caucasus, amongst oak woods and green hills.

At Batoum once again I took ship, coasting the eastern and northern shores of the Black Sea, touching at various points of interest, such as Kertch and Sebastopol.

It was the 6th of July when we reached Odessa, and it was with feelings of singular satisfaction on the evening of that day that I took my ticket for London, and " wished myself there."

INDEX.

Achtagh, 212.
Akar, or female Ovis—see *Ovis poli.*
Ak Masjid, 42, 43.
Aksak Maral, 145.
Aksu, the city of, 162—residence at, 206—a court of justice at, *ib.*
Ak-Tapa, 273.
Amban, the, of Yarkand, 129, 132 *et seq.*
Antelopes, 6, 19, 32.
Araba, or country cart, 140.
Arpalik Dawan, the, 57.

Baku, 274.
Bashkiok, 170—the houses at, *ib.*
Batoum, 274.
Battery, a, 24—arrangement of, 25.
Bish-arik, 272.
Böghe, or stag, 110, 145, 151.
Borakatai, 229.
Bower, Captain, 22 *et passim.*
Burrel-shooting, 6, 13.

Camel-steak, 172.
Camels, wild, 171, 172, 177, 178.
Camp-life, the three necessaries of, 35.
Carawul Pass, 32.
"Carolini" sheep, 196, 219, 221.
Chaddirtash, 97, 102, 108.
Charcken, 181, 184.
Charlung valley, the, 116.
Charoks, 137, 139, 151.
Charwagh, 157.

Chilas, 7.
Chillon, 160.
Chinaman, a friendly visit from a, 150.
Chinese character, good point in, 144.
Chinese coins, 139.
Chinese soldiers, insolence of, 207, 208—administering a moral lesson to, 208, 209—an amicable settlement, 210.
Chinese Turkistan, preparing to start for, 21—securing a guide, 23—laying in stores for the journey, 24, 29—the inhabitants of, 143.
Chinese way of drinking tea, 134.
Chini Pass, 5.
Chuplies, 137 and note.
Clothes, mistakes travellers in the East make as to, 64.
"Coolen" (*Grus cinerea*), 123.
Crushnai, successful ibex-shooting in, 16.

Dad Mahomed, 27, 32, 54, 128, 129, 180—capture of, 224-227.
Dagshai, 13.
Dauvergne, M., 27 *et passim.*
Dawan-Urtang, the, 41.
Deer-drive, a, 205.
Depsang plains, 18.
Digar La, 17.
Douglas, Major Johnstone, 25, 26, 27.

INDEX.

Drivers, trouble with, 34.
Dusterkhan, a, 53, 65, 67, 135.

Eagle, hunting with a trained, 167-170.
Eastern Turkistan, the plain of, 120.
Egizarak Kurgaon, 57.

Farghana plains, 267, 269.

Gaomukhi, or Cow's Mouth, 11, 13.
Goatskin raft, a, 58 *et seq.*
Gond, 26.
Goolja, or male Ovis—see *Ovis poli*.
Gorges, fine, 57, 58, 59, 118.
Grass-shoe, a, 4 and note.
Graveyard in the desert, a, 173.
Gromchefski, Russian explorer, 97—curious conversation with, 108.
Gya, 19.

Hakim Beg, 58, 59—his excitability, 60—the viceregal lodge of, 65.
Hemmis, festival at the *gompa* or monastery of, 17.
Henry .500-bore muzzle-loader the best weapon for mountain-shooting, 6, 7 — a double barrel a dangerous weapon for a beginner, 7.
Hot springs, fishing in, 111.

Ibex, first day shooting, 3 *et seq.*—a good record, 16—a herd of, 107.
"Imperial grouse," 222.

Jai Dubba, 221.
Jeran, stalking a, 146 — hunting, with an eagle, 167, 168—a good shot at, 202.
Jizak, 273.

Kalmuk country, the, 188 — the people of, 189—their habits and religion, *ib.*—applying for a guide, 191, 192—Ovis in the hills, 195—intense cold, *ib.*
Kalmuki camps, 194, 195.
Kalmuki guide, engaging a, 191.
Kalti Ailak, 222.
Kangan, 26.
Karaat Pass, 239.
Kara Dawan, or black pass, 117.

Karachunkar Pass, 75.
Karakoram, 18, 32, 267.
Karakul Pamir, the, 240 *et seq.*
Karim Khan, 233, 240, 241, 243, 252, 255.
Kashgar, 223 *et seq.*
Kashmir, 2, 7.
Kashmiri servants, accommodating character of, 74.
Kaufmann Peak, 240.
Khan of Kalmuk, the mother of the, 197.
Khardung Pass, 29.
Khargoshi Pamir, 240, 247.
Khojend, 272.
Khokand, 272.
Khotan Kama, 167.
Kilian Pass, the, 33.
Kilik valley, 94, 95, 99.
Kirghiz *yurts* or tents, 34 *et passim.*
Kitchikul Pass, 43.
Kizil Art Pass, 259, 262.
Kizil Dawan, or red pass, 117, 118.
Kizilean river, 263.
Kobrang valley, 6.
Kosh-beli Pass, 234.
Kuchar, 180, 181.
Kugiar, 46, 48.
Kunjerat Pass, the, 103.
Kurla, 185.
Kutch Mahomed, 75, 102.

Lammergeirs, 95.
Langar, 58.
Leh, 6, 17, 19, 27.
Littledale, Mr and Mrs, 261.

Mahomed Amin, 164, 211, 213.
Mahomed Unis, 118, 125, 126, 128, 130, 132—the dwelling of, 135, 136.
Mangal nullah, fatal accident in, 15, 16.
Maralbashi, 130, 134, 138, 141, 155.
Marghilan, 269, 271.
Markhor, a splendid herd of, 9—a good stalk, *ib.*—trying for, 22.
Marsemik Pass, 6.
Mintaka, 102, 112.

Native, a friendly, 42.
Nubra valley, 17, 31.

INDEX.

Ovis *Ammon*, 6, 19—an easy stalk, 20.
Ovis *poli*, or Marco Polo's sheep, 2, 48—first signs of, 71—a herd of, 77, 79—a fine shot at, spoiled by a wolf, 80—meat of, 86—a herd spotted, 87—successful stalking of, 88, 91—hard work hunting, 94—disappointing shots, 96, 99, 100—another herd sighted, 103—a good day's work at, 104, 105—a herd of akars, 218—a broadside at, *ib.*—sighting a herd, 235—a long watch for, *ib.*—a bad shot, 238—gooljas in sight, 242 *et seq.*—tracking and stalking, 246-261.

Pamirs, the, journey to, 37-85—a snowstorm in, 86 *et seq.*
Panamikh, 31.
Pangi, expedition to, 5—success at, 6.
Pargarma Peak, 70.
Parting, a sad, 266.
Partridges (*Perdrix barbatus*), 214.
Pheasants, a beat for, 148.
Pilgrim, a timorous, 12.
Pir Panjal, the, 14.
Ponies, arranging for, 24—a mishap to, 26—objecting to be saddled, 29—trying work for, 39—buying, 56—novel work for, 61—a fearful cropper to one of the, 69—great difficulty with, 114—bleeding the nostrils of, considered an infallible restorative, 115—a herd of, 116—hiring a team, 138—fording a river, 231—death of one of the, 234—taking French leave, 262.
Potash gorge, 19.

Ramsay, Captain, 27.
Red bears, 3.
Rupel glacier, the, 8.
Russian expedition, a, 44, 153.
Russian merchants, 165.

Salti, 30.
Sambur, 13.
Sanju Kurgaon, 33.
Saragat Pass, the, 38.
Sasar Pass, difficult roads over the, 17, 32.

Scent, effect and spread of, 85.
Shah Yar, 178, 180, 181, 199.
Shamal, 149, 151.
Shapoo, 20.
Sheep, the droppings of, used for fuel, 93.
Shyok river, 17, 18—valley, 30.
Sirikul Pamir, 73.
Snow-cocks, 214, 215.
Soutan, 215.
Srinagar, 5, 22.
Stag-shooting, 151 *et seq.*—a tempting shot, 178, 179.
Sultan Beg, 55, 56, 57.

Taghar, 31.
Taghdumbash, 70, 71, 73.
Taghdumbash Pamir, 63, 73, 103.
Tagherma Peak, 113, 114.
Tahr (*Hemitragus jemlaicus*), 22.
Tahta Dawan, 56.
Takla Makhan, the legend of, 175, 176.
Tashkurgan, the Beg of, 72—the fort of, 73.
Tashkurgan river, 75, 107, 113.
Tengiz-bai Pass, 267.
Terrek Langar, 142.
Thornton, Colonel, 20.
Tian Shan mountains, 157, 162, 166, 186, 188, 212.
Tigers, a pair of marauding, 183, 184.
Tiznaf river, fishing in the, 52.
Tiznaf valley, 49, 50.
Torak Pass, 115.
Tumchuk, 158.
Tung, 59, 63, 64.
Turkistan, the universal custom in, 124.
Tusla Dawan, the, 39.

Uch Kurghan, 269.
Ura-Tapa, 272.
Ushlaich, the village of, 52.
Ushturfan, 211, 212.
Uyoung, 53.

Wahab Jilga, 18.
Wakhis, a camp of, 37—their hospitality, *ib.*, 38.
Water-fowl, 200, 203.
Wolves destructive to poli, 82, 94.

Yakka, 182.
Yaks, shooting, 6—procuring a team of, 40, 69.
Yangi-Shahar, or Chinese town of Yarkand, 125.
Yarkand, journey to, 110 *et seq.*— *karaol* or outpost of, 121—appearance of the town, 125—residence at, 127—the city of, on a market-day, 130—the Chinese quarter of, 131—Amban of, 132 *et seq.*—milestones of, 141.
Younghusband, Major, 108, 111, 112.
Yulduz, 186.

THE END.

www.ingramcontent.com/pod-product-compliance
Lightning Source LLC
Chambersburg PA
CBHW032111230426
43672CB00009B/1702